Ethan
Levinskas

YOU KNOW YOU'RE A
DRAGON BALL Z FANATIC IF...

...you think your teacher is a Saiyan

...you name your dog "Bubbles" and make
him bounce around your backyard "planet"
at rocketship speed

...you insist that your power level is 1200
(on bad days)

...you wear red pajamas and a sash to school

...you blow grapefruits across the cafeteria,
claiming to be Frieza or Nappa

Dragon Ball Z

An Unauthorized Guide

Lois and Danny Gresh

St. Martin's Paperbacks

DRAGON BALL Z: AN UNAUTHORIZED GUIDE

Copyright © 2000 by Lois H. Gresh and Danny N. Gresh.

All rights reserved. No part of this book may be used or reproduced in any manner whatsoever without written permission except in the case of brief quotations embodied in critical articles or reviews. For information address St. Martin's Press, 175 Fifth Avenue, New York, N.Y. 10010.

ISBN: 0-312-97757-3

Printed in the United States of America

St. Martin's Paperbacks edition / August 2000

10 9 8 7 6 5 4 3 2 1

Dedicated with love to the people who care: Rena, Grandma, and Uncle Mark. Special love to Grandpa.

—Lois H. Gresh and Danny N. Gresh

Many thanks to our agent, Lori Perkins, and to our editor, Marc Resnick. Also, our thanks go to Mr. Yutaka Morita, who kindly translated Japanese trading cards into English for us.

Table of Contents

1

So What's It All About?

"This may be better than Pokémon. There's more action."
—Danny Gresh, 10 years old and coauthor of this book

"This is very funny and very exciting, too."
—Matt, 11 years old

"Forget fighting, give me a math test!"
—Definitely not Gohan

Apart, they're just seven magic balls. But if you find them and bring them together, they summon The Eternal Dragon . . .

. . . *who rises from his lair in a fury of ageless wonder and grants a secret wish to the person who woke him up.*

Cool, huh? That's what Dragon Ball Z is all about, and it stars Goku, a boy with a tail who comes to Earth from a distant planet called Vegeta. He's raised by a master of martial arts, and his training coupled with his awesome Super Saiyan powers make him the strongest man on Earth.

But the Saiyans are super strong, too. They come back to conquer Earth and to blow away everyone on the planet. They want to find the seven dragon balls so they can summon The Eternal Dragon and ask for immortality—to live forever. There's Vegeta, the Prince of all Saiyans, and his really nasty sidekick, Nappa.

*"Nappa's worse than all the bad guys on
World Wrestling put together."*
—Eric, 10 years old

But Vegeta and Nappa and Goku are just the beginning of the cartoon adventure called Dragon Ball Z. It's on TV every day (check the Cartoon Network in your town or city). In addition, there have been numerous movies featuring lots of favorite Dragon Ball Z characters.

We've seen every available episode and movie.

Have you? If so, then you're as hooked on Dragon Ball Z as we are, which means that you're a fan on the level of Super Saiyan Fan, if such a thing could exist. It also means we'll have a good time in this book. We'll find out what you like best—the characters, the episodes, the sagas. And you'll find out what we like best, and why.

We'll tell you how the show was created—who the genius was behind all this great stuff, and how he created all those super mean guys and all those great Dragon Ball Z jokes.

If you're not all that familiar with the television show, we'll tell you what's so exciting, and so hysterically funny, about the adventures and characters in the various episodes.

Here's what Danny says about the action and comedy of Dragon Ball Z:

"It's really amazing how they get all that action and all that funny stuff on one TV show. Like when some nasty guy calls Krillin a 'near-sighted cueball head' and how they have aircars and dinosaurs together. One of the funniest parts is when Goku trains with King Kai, who doubles as a martial arts master and comedian. King Kai makes Goku laugh at all his jokes, and he also makes Goku chase his monkey, Bubbles, all over the planet in heavy gravity."

This happens during the thirteenth episode of Dragon Ball Z, which is called "A Fight Against Gravity . . . Catch Bubbles!"

Now I like catching bubbles, but only if they're in my ginger ale or bathtub. I wouldn't like chasing a monkey round and round a planet that's the size of a giant grapefruit or something. Especially a monkey who spins like a top, goes backward, and is so heavy that he can crush a car by jumping on it.

I guess now is a good time to tell you who "I" am and who "Danny" is. I am writing this book. My name is Lois. Danny is my kid. The two of us have been playing together forever. When he was little, we made giant construction sites in the mud behind our house. We drove giant trucks all over our construction sites. We found hundreds of ladybugs in our flowers. Now we play lots of baseball, watch cartoons, play with action figures and board games, and he may not want to admit it to you, but we like to play chess, too. I guess you could say we like doing the same things.

We have pretty much all the Donald Duck comic books. And lots of adventure stories, like cowboy novels, old science fiction thrillers, Tom Swift, and the Hardy Boys. We like to read adventure books, so it's natural that we'd write something like Dragon Ball Z. Speaking of which, this Dragon Ball Z book is probably one of the best books you'll ever read, but there are lots of other good books out there, too. So if you're reading this book, go read another one when you're done!

Well, as I mentioned, Danny and I like cartoons. Not like the Flintstones (which I watched when I was a little girl and it's okay), but more like Dragon Ball Z, where the action keeps going from episode to episode, and you have to keep watching to find out what's going to happen next. We both like to laugh a lot, too, and Dragon Ball Z is pretty funny.

Being a mother, I like Gohan. I keep worrying

that he's going to be killed or hurt badly. I get so scared! Being a kid, Danny doesn't know why I worry about Gohan and why I sometimes get scared during fight scenes. "It's just a cartoon, Mom!" That's what Danny says to me all the time. (His friend, Eric, says, "Danny, your Mom is *so* weird.")

Danny and Eric like Vegeta, plus any character who's eating like a pig right at that moment.

I like Oolong, who's a pig, but that's only because I sleep with two stuffed pigs, Cal and Oinky, who are now famous because they're in this book.

Danny often catches me playing with Cal and Oinky, and also with my action figures. I have zombie action figures and all sorts of monsters—they're my favorites. But I also like to play with Goku, Piccolo, Gohan, and Vegeta. It may seem silly that a grown woman plays with this stuff, but I know another grown woman who does just the same thing, so I'm not the only one. And she has a kid Danny's age, too.

So that's who Danny and I are, and now you know why we're writing this book: we're nuts about Dragon Ball Z. We invite you to come and meet us at *http://www.sff.net/people/lgresh/*

Dragon BallZ.html, where we hang out with other kids and talk about Dragon Ball Z stuff. Danny's there all the time . . .

Except when he's in school or doing homework . . . or practicing his trumpet, or playing hockey or baseball . . . or . . .

Listen, trust me, he's there an awful lot! I'm his mother, I should know!

Anyway, if you are on the Internet, go to that address and say hello to us. We have Dragon Ball Z pictures and information there. For example, you can see photos of Danny writing about action figures while playing with them on his desk.

Speaking of which, want to know how a kid just like you writes a book chapter? This was Danny's step-by-step process:

1. Played with Piccolo, Vegeta, and Captain Ginyu
2. Turned to the computer, typed some paragraphs about how he made Ginyu attack the other two and which guy lost which body parts
3. Played with Thin and Fat Majin Buu
4. Wrote some Buu suggestions and comments
5. Played some more
6. Played some more . . .

And, well, I think he just kept playing with the action figures and stopped writing the chapter.

Also on the Website, you can see photos of Danny working on the role-playing game chapter, and Danny studying Dragon Ball Z comics to give you important research tips. For example, here's an important research tip straight from the comics: if you're Piccolo in a role-playing game, you should say "Feh!" a lot. This is Piccolo's favorite word.

The only way to learn this important fact about being Piccolo in a role-playing game is to study the comic books until midnight. Well, that's what Danny tells me every night . . .

Danny posts many fascinating Dragon Ball Z facts on the Website. For example, by studying the comic books, he realized that there are many names for the famous Piccolo attack. I call it the screwdriver attack. That's what the Piccolo action figure has as his power weapon: a big screwdriver. But I know that's not the real name of the attack. In the comics, they call it "The Light Beam of Death," which is kind of melodramatic, don't you think? In the cartoon, they call it "Special Beam Cannon." And it's called something like Makkankaposo in the Ani-Mayhem card game, which you can't find anymore (a real bummer and near-crime that should be remedied right away). Danny calls it the corkscrew attack. He's probably right.

See how my mind is? I start talking about one aspect of Dragon Ball Z, such as our Website, and then my brain flies out like a fishing line into some ocean, and I drag out some totally different tidbit about Dragon Ball Z. Then I start talking about this new tidbit, such as Danny reading the comics, and bam, I float right back into the ocean and reel in a tidbit about Piccolo action figures and all the names of Piccolo's special energy attack.

Once you get hooked on this stuff, it's hard to stop and take a deep breath—one of those great big breaths we're all supposed to take when we get really excited about something and other people want us to slow down. It's hard to say to ourselves, "Okay, that's enough about Dragon Ball Z."

We're just too *hooked*.

Anyway, please come to the Website and tell us what you like about Dragon Ball Z. Also, we're dying to know what you think about this book, so come to *http://www.sff.net/people/lgresh/DragonballZ.html* and tell us.

We end each chapter of this book with a Fast Fact Quiz. All the quizzes are secret standardized

tests by the National Teachers Union to determine your IQ. If you flunk the quizzes in this
book, the National Teachers Union will instantly
demote you to nursery school, where you'll be
forced to play Foxy Woxy in Chicken Little
plays for the rest of your life. So be really careful
and use a number two pencil. Mark your answers
clearly, and then double-check your answers.

Okay, I bet you're scared half out of your wits
by the thought of these hard quizzes. Calm down,
be cool. I swear: these quizzes are a piece of
cake! Here's an example:

Fast Fact Quiz!

Which character uses the Don Demo Mizuu ni Kaeteshimau non Royoko attack?

Answer 1: Piccolo

Answer 2: Aqua

Answer 3: Kami Sami Piccolo Whammy

Answer 4: George the Fish

Easy, huh? Oh, whoops, wait a minute. That's not one of the quiz questions. It could be, and the real answer is #2, but such a quiz question would flunk you straight back to nursery school for sure. We wouldn't do that to you. But we might ask you this one:

Fast Fact Quiz!

Which character uses the Bad Breath attack?

Answer 1: Evil Majin Buu, who can destroy an entire city with his breath

Answer 2: Salami, the talking dolphin, who can destroy an entire ocean with his gills

Answer 3: the Bulbous Dodo, an extinct bird species derived from carnivorous dinosaurs and which once devoured the plains of Kansas before being destroyed by wolves

Answer 4: George the Fish

The correct answer is #1. See? You just learned something true about Evil Majin Buu by taking a very tricky test. We'll report your amazing accomplishment to the National Teachers Union. You can't lose with this book! That's what happens when you read books written by 10-year-old kids.

If you don't know the answers, we even give you a cheat sheet—see Appendix B.

Of course, you can't trust us about the answers. For example, we told you that Evil Majin Buu has a Bad Breath attack, and that's not entirely true. I believe in the deepest recesses of my heart—as opposed to the most shallow recesses of my liver—that Buu's breath stinks. I will now explain, and you can decide for yourself.

From an official perspective, Majin Buu's attack is called Breath rather than Bad Breath. Now let's look at the facts. Buu turns people into candy and cookies, and then he eats them. If Danny ate that much candy and that many cookies, he'd get 245 cavities; all of the teeth in his head would drop onto the floor. And his breath would stink.

So why should Majin Buu be any different? Clearly, a guy who eats nothing but human-sized candy is going to have at least 245 cavities, if he has any teeth left at all. And he's going to have really bad breath. If you don't trust me on this, ask your dentist and he'll tell you!

That's enough about bad breath. It's time to put on your purple horns and strike a pose. It's time to hold onto your seat and tickle your toes (but keep one hand free to turn the pages). It's going to be a wild ride, as we blast off into the mega-fun world of Dragon Ball Z!

Fast Fact Quiz!
(the real one at the end of this chapter)

A yoikominiminkminiminken is a:

Answer 1: ridiculous make-believe name of an
attack

Answer 2: power-up maneuver

Answer 3: flash of power from millions of tiny
cannons

Answer 4: word for many egg yolks in Japanese

2

A Short History of Dragon Ball Z

"Why do these Dragon Ball Z videos claim to have brief nudity in them? Does that mean the uncut episodes show Gohan fall naked from the sky after he transforms back from the Giant Monkey?"
—Danny Gresh, 10 years old and coauthor of this book

"I think so. What else can it mean? It's a Dragon Ball Z cartoon. Maybe the brief nudity is when Goku's shirt gets ripped in a fight."
—Lois Gresh (Me)

"Maybe it means that Vegeta's pants fall down."
—Danny

"I don't think so. That's highly unlikely. I mean, this is a Dragon Ball Z cartoon. What kind of stuff could be in it that requires parental warnings?"
—Me

"I think it means they spit out blood and that the blood is briefly nude."
—Dan

"Uh-huh. Well, I will watch this uncut Dragon Ball Z cartoon alone before you get to watch it. Just to make sure there's nothing horrible in it. Oh brother. On second thought, we can watch it together. There just *can't* be any nudity in a Dragon Ball Z cartoon. This is ridiculous . . . But if I yell, 'DAN HIDE YOUR EYES,' immediately put this pillow on your face."
—Me

"Okay, Mom, but I'll use Cal instead. He's big. I'll stick Cal on my face if something nude happens."
—Dan

[later after my stuffed pig, Cal, gets an hour-long workout . . .]

"Uncut with brief nudity means they spit out some blood and that the blood is briefly nude. Oh, and that Gohan falls from the sky in the faraway distance after he transforms back

from the Giant Monkey. THERE'S NO NEED TO
HIDE YOUR EYES BEHIND A STUFFED PIG
WHILE WATCHING DRAGON BALL Z
EPISODES."
—Me

Okay, I got a little carried away with the introductory quotes. But I thought that information was important and that you needed to know it right away. After all, in Japan, brief nudity means that a cartoon might show a naked Giant Monkey, which of course, is naked except for its fur. And then when the Monkey transforms back into a little boy, the boy probably doesn't have much fur covering his flesh. And we do see him from behind, which means literally that we see his behind.

You have now learned another important fact that the National Teachers Union will care about a lot.

Everyone we know says that the creator of Dragon Ball Z, the cartoon genius named Akira Toriyama, has a terrific sense of humor. When he started with the original Dragon Ball series, which I'll tell you about in a minute, he stuffed in lots of toilet jokes and silliness. Danny once thought that maybe Akira Toriyama wrote the original Dragon Ball cartoons when he was potty training his kid.

Highly unlikely, but then I was wrong about the meaning of uncut episodes and Danny was right. Danny is sometimes much smarter about these things than I am.

Now—only because I feel that I have to regain my big smartie status as the older coauthor here—I will tell you a little bit about the creator of Dragon Ball Z, why he created the series, and when he first started working on it.

Answers to these questions have become Dragon Ball Z lore. That creates a question: what's lore?

Some of you already know the answer. I will ask Dan.

"Dan, do you know what the word 'lore' means?"

"Uh, I think I've heard of it in some video games." (He names a specific video game here, but I will omit it because it doesn't happen to be a Dragon Ball Z video game.)

Me: "But what does it mean? *Lore*." (I'm feeling like a really big smartie right now.)

Dan: "Is it sort of like *lure*?"

Me: "No, guess again."

Dan: "I don't know. Is it a dung beetle?"

Now I have to point out that Danny gets lots

of A's on his report card in school and knows the meanings of enormous and very bizarre vocabulary words. Here's an example that he told me about just tonight while we were driving to Super Shack Haircuts to get his dog-fur-mutt-hairdo trimmed: "Arachabutyrophobia. It means fear of getting peanut butter stuck to the roof of your mouth."

Here's another one: "Triskaidekaphobia. It means fear of the number thirteen."

So if you don't know the meaning of the word "lore" don't feel bad. (And now I'm feeling like a bad mother because Danny doesn't know the meaning of the word, but then again, I'm just like that . . . hopefully, I'm not as bad as Gohan's mother, ChiChi.)

Simply put, lore means legend, gospel, something that we all seem to know without thinking about it. For example, anyone who's watched Dragon Ball Z a few times knows that all bad guys want the dragon balls. After you've watched the show a few dozen times, or after you've read a pile of the comics, you also know that ChiChi likes to dress Gohan in weird clothes and make him study a lot. (I must defend myself. I do not make Danny study a lot. I do not make Danny wear weird clothes.) These sorts of facts are all part of the Dragon Ball Z lore.

To learn more about the history and creation of the actual cartoon show and comics, which in turn gave us the action figures and trading cards, the first thing you need to know is that there was a series called Dragon Ball *before* Dragon Ball Z and that there was a series called Dragon Ball GT *after* Dragon Ball Z.

Another thing you need to know—and we've hinted at this already—is that Dragon Ball Z exists as a manga series, which means comics, as well as an anime, or cartoon. We'll tell you about the comics, as well as the cartoon episodes, later in this book.

First, let's get back to our short history of Dragon Ball Z.

Once you've seen a photo of Akira Toriyama, the creator of Dragon Ball, you never forget him. You instantly think, *Wow, what a great guy!* Then you want to find out as much as you can about him. Luckily, you can learn a lot about Akira Toriyama just by cruising around the Internet.

Akira Toriyama created the original Dragon Ball series in 1985. The original series aired approximately 153 cartoon episodes. Dragon Ball was cute and humorous, and of course, filled with adventures. It also aired several movies.

Later came Dragon Ball Z, which aired hundreds of episodes and three movies. Dragon Ball Z isn't as airy with humor as its predecessor, Dragon Ball. Instead, Dragon Ball Z focuses on action and adventure, good guys versus bad guys, right versus wrong.

Together, Dragon Ball and Dragon Ball Z include 42 Japanese black-and-white comic books. In America, translated versions of the Japanese Dragon Ball Z comics are published by a place called Viz Select Comics.

Dragon Ball GT (which stands for Grand Tour) is the last series in the Dragon Ball saga. It started appearing on Japanese television in early 1996.

All together, Danny and I think that there are 519 episodes of Dragon Ball, Dragon Ball Z, and Dragon Ball GT. We don't generally sit around counting cartoon episodes, but we're sure that the number is way up there in the many, many hundreds. A lot of these episodes are only in Japanese, and fans in America, Canada, England, Spain, and all over the world keep begging and hoping for subtitled or dubbed versions.

According to Dragon Ball Z lore, Akira Toriyama was watching Jackie Chan movies right before he came up with the idea behind the original Dragon Ball series. He wanted to write a manga series about a boy who does a lot of kung fu fighting. Of course, as in all good kung fu films and books, the bad guys had to get stronger over time and harder to beat, and the good guys had to become increasingly better fighters.

Now if you're like Dan and me, you like anything that has to do with kung fu fighting. I also think ninjas are pretty cool, too, but they have little to do with Dragon Ball Z. I'll digress for only one moment to mention that Ninjas can cling with their hands to ceilings as if they are attached by suckers. They can also run straight up tree trunks. They have more than 80 secret hand maneuvers. Or so I've heard.

So ninjas make very interesting Dragon Ball Z characters. However, so do kung fu fighters, and we all know that Dragon Ball Z is crammed with tons of kung fu fighters.

A long pole is a staple of kung fu fighting. Goku uses a long pole in many of his fights. With the pole behind his head and across his shoulders, the fighter places his hands far apart on the pole. By practicing body movements with the pole positioned like this, the fighter learns to keep his shoulders straight as he moves. This means that he can deliver more powerful punches by using both shoulders instead of one.

Some of the key things taught to people who are learning martial arts like kung fu fighting are:

- Being fast on your feet is really important
- An excellent fighter shifts his body to avoid most attacks
- An excellent fighter has a body that seems very light
- An excellent fighter moves like a stallion, fast but graceful

Are you starting to see a theme? Fast on your feet, move so fast you avoid all blows, fast and graceful, body seems really light. These all sound like descriptions of Goku's moves in Dragon Ball Z. He works out in heavy gravity so his body can feel very light. He's so fast as a Human-Saiyan that you don't see him move. He's so fast as a Super Saiyan that he avoids all blows.

Another key factor in kung fu fighting (and all martial arts) is that a person's mind can enhance his physical strength. What this means is that if you focus hard enough on the positive flow of your own energy and abilities, you will be much stronger during a hard battle.

This is actually a good fact to remember no matter what you're doing in life. I wish that I could remember it more often.

For example, if you think that you're a lousy ball player, then you *will* be a lousy ball player. If, on the other hand, you tell yourself that you can smack a baseball into the outfield, chances are that you'll get good enough to do it. If you tell yourself that you can't run two miles, you'll walk and never build the strength to run even one mile. If, on the other hand, you tell yourself that you *can* run two miles, you'll work up to it quickly and become much stronger in the process.

In Dragon Ball Z, as in martial arts, this inner brain power that makes you stronger is known as *ki*. It's a flowing energy that rises inside a person, becomes very focused, and enables the person to work harder, work longer, and achieve great physical and mental strength. It flows constantly in cycles throughout our bodies and brains.

It really does work. The more you drive yourself, the harder you strive to do a great job, the better you'll do in all aspects of life. You know how your parents and teachers say, "Always do your best." They're telling you in simple terms to channel your inner ki in a positive way.

Dragon Ball Z characters channel their ki constantly—in every comic and every cartoon adventure. After each battle, they tend to grow in ki and in overall physical power. That's why their power levels keep rising throughout the series. The harder they work, the better they get.

Isn't that cool? When I first started watching

Dragon Ball Z, this thought didn't occur to me, and I was confused about why the characters' power levels kept rising after every fight. Dan and I figured that it was because the cartoons had to go on and on, and the only way to keep the show truly exciting was to keep increasing everyone's power levels. Then I started thinking about the meaning of ki and Dragon Ball Z's use of martial arts techniques, and it all made sense.

In the Japanese language, the word *do* means *the way of*. In Chinese, the word *dao* (Mandarin) or *doe* (Cantonese) means *the creative force governing all of nature* or *the force in nature that makes all things*. These words are all very similar. When coupled with other words, they relate to the use of ki. For example, judo is the way of gentleness, and *aikido* is the way of harmonizing the ki.

I think that King Kai's name comes directly from this interpretation. Let's face it: his name is King *Kai*, and he's the master or all-powerful king of channeling ki. I may be wrong about King Kai's name, but it seems a likely guess.

There are actually martial arts exercises that help fighters increase their channeling of ki. These exercises enable people to remain relaxed without sacrificing their power during fights.

King Kai spends his life teaching guys like

Goku how to channel their ki using martial arts exercises. There does seem to be a distinct connection between King Kai and the fundamental meaning of ki.

In real life, kung fu guys also think that we can summon all the raging anger inside us and channel it into physical strength. This is what Gohan does as a four-year-old boy. When Gohan gets fiercely angry because somebody seems to have killed Krillin, Piccolo, or Goku, he amasses stunning amounts of physical power based solely on his inner force. You know how he screws up his face and grunts right before he explodes in anger and hurls some huge power ball at the bad guys? That's Gohan taking all his raging anger and channeling it into physical strength. Pure ki. Pure martial arts. Pure Dragon Ball Z.

One basic exercise in real martial arts is to imagine that energy is flowing from your bellybutton up your body and down your arms. You should feel that the bottoms of your arms are heavy. You pretend that all the energy is flowing out your fingers. When you get really good at this exercise, opponents won't be able to move your elbows or make your arms move toward your body. Martial arts masters can use their ki force to strike a powerful blow by twisting their fist up one inch. That's it. Up one inch, and their opponents are hurled through the air and to the floor.

Ever notice how Dragon Ball Z characters focus forever before throwing an energy blast? Ever notice how the energy blasts stream from their hands? Goku, Krillin, Piccolo, Vegeta, Gohan, and all the others are focusing their ki before releasing it from their fingertips or hands. In standard kung fu fashion.

Ignore for now the maniacs like Frieza who blast energy beams from their mouths. They are sick weirdos. Or maybe guys like Frieza have a special alien kung fu technique for focusing their ki, such as blowing it up their tails and then out their mouths. It might be different for creatures with tails.

Another obvious martial arts technique in Dragon Ball Z is the kick. Everyone's always kicking everybody else. It is thought in martial arts circles that an excellent kick is the most powerful blow. Because legs are longer than arms, fighters tend to kick first, then follow up with a punch. Speed and power are essential, of course, and in Dragon Ball Z, the guys start kicking so fast and with so much power you can't see their legs! Whip whip whiz whiz, these kicking scenes are some of the funniest and most entertaining in all of Dragon Ball Z.

It's also funny when guys like Recoome lose half their hair during a particularly difficult battle. Or when Recoome actually gains teeth during a fight rather than losing teeth, as most people do when some macho guy clobbers them in the face.

Another notion essential to martial arts is that the fighter should be pliable yet assertive and hard. Rather than fight force with force, the martial arts expert bends under the opponent's force, lets the opponent use up all his fighting power. Then, when his opponent is weak from expending all that energy, the martial arts expert strikes a powerful blow.

Thus, he's pliable, bending, soft; this is when he lets the opponent get all worn out from attacking him. When the time's right, when the opponent is weak, the good kung fu fighter attacks; he becomes assertive and hard.

Goku uses this soft-hard technique all the time. He dodges blows, he even seems bored at times. The other guy gets tired from attacking him. That's when Goku attacks.

When discussing this pliable yet assertive-hard stuff, kung fu fighters talk about water a lot. It's a common analogy. Water is soft, formless, and flows forever. It's the fighter in his pliable and soft state: unbreakable.

Water also shows up constantly in Dragon Ball Z. Oceans part, floods rise from the sea, craters are blasted into solid ground and instantly fill with tidal waves. Dragon Ball Z is filled with water, water, and more water.

I think that's because Akira Toriyama was heavily into kung fu movies when he decided to create Dragon Ball Z. And water is a major way of talking about ki and the flow of internal energy in the kung fu world.

The final thing I'll point out about martial arts is that excellent fighters learn to see in many directions at once. This is called peripheral vision. They train with special exercises so they can see attackers coming from all angles. They focus on an object in the distance. While maintaining their sharp gaze on the object, they also start focusing on everything around the object. Specifically, training is best when the fighter gazes at people rather than objects. This way, the fighter can focus on one person while noting the movements of other people circling around him from different directions.

Fascinating insight by Dan: "What about dragons? Kung fu fighting films are about dragons, aren't they? Just like Dragon Ball Z."

True enough, and a good point. I seem to remember that Dan and I have seen various kung fu dragon films together.

Bruce Lee, a famous martial arts fighter, starred in a series of dragon-related kung fu films. *Enter the Dragon, The Way of the Dragon*, and *Return of the Dragon*. There may be others, I do not recall. I also know that in China, the Hour of the Dragon is between six and eight o'clock in the morning. So I think that Danny makes a good point that dragons must be a popular component to kung fu television and movies.

Dragon Ball Z follows that tradition, as well as the traditional thinking about ki. Remember when the small dragon befriends Gohan? That's a minor dragon compared to the two *huge* dragons that perform feats of wonder on both Earth and Namek. And then there's Snake Way, the Dragon Ball Z bridge between life and death— called The Other Dimension in Dragon Ball Z.

In real Chinese mythology, Eternal Dragons are also the bridge between life and death, which is known as The Other World. Pretty similar to Dragon Ball Z, don't you think? Not only that, in real Chinese mythology, The Eternal Dragons work with wise Guardians who help us learn how to become stronger and better people. Dragon Ball Z's most famous Guardian is Kami.

In addition to kung fu fighting, the Dragon

Ball Z lore tells us that Akira Toriyama wanted to base the series, which started as comic books, on the ancient Chinese legend of the monkey king. At one time, he was actually going to make Goku a monkey. Instead, he made Goku into a human boy with a tail. The tail was the only part of the monkey that stayed with Goku, at least in his human form. All Saiyans with tails can turn into Giant Monkeys when the moon is full.

The Monkey King Legend, which was written approximately 400 years ago, is also known as Journey to the West. It's an extremely famous Chinese legend. I went to the bookstore to find a copy, figuring that the legend would be a couple dozen pages long. No way! The Monkey King Legend was published in four giant volumes. This is a *very long* famous Chinese legend. It was written by Wu Cheng'en in the 1500's.

Basically, the legend is based on the true story of a Chinese monk named Xuan Zang, who lived between the years 602 and 664 A.D. He walked all the way from Great Tang, which is what they called China in the early 600's, to India. He was looking for a Buddhist holy book called the Sutra.

The Monkey King Legend is a *very long* but entertaining tale about Xuan Zang's journey into India and then back to Great Tang. It includes

Chinese fairy tales and superstitions, and all sorts of monster stories and adventures.

In the legend, the Monkey King isn't quite human. Well, he's not very human at all—he was born from a rock egg.

He learns all sorts of tricks and kung fu type stuff, and eventually figures out how to shape-shift himself into 72 different objects. For example, the Monkey King might look like a bug or a tree.

He uses clouds to travel quickly through the sky, going as fast as 180,000 miles per hour. He eats peaches of immortality, which oddly enough, remind me of dragon balls.

As you might guess, the Monkey King engages in many fights. Nobody can defeat him. They go so far as to try to burn the Monkey King in a furnace, but rather than killing him, the flames give the Monkey King burning golden eyes. They go so far as to topple a mountain on him, but of course, he survives that, too. But he gets stuck under the mountain, and it's only when Xuan Zang shows up 500 years later that the Monkey King gets free again.

Other guys go with the Monkey King, as he and Xuan Zang travel and have adventures, seeking the holy Sutra. One guy is a funny but timid pig who is thrown out of heaven for assaulting a fairy. Another guy is a dragon horse.

It must be pretty obvious by now why we said that Dragon Ball Z is a lot like the Monkey King Legend. As noted earlier, Goku is based on the Monkey King himself. Goku's flying nimbus is based on the clouds that the Monkey King uses to fly at 180,000 miles per hour. Oolong is the funny but timid pig who accompanies the Monkey King and Xuan Zang during their adventures seeking the Sutra. Oolong is also a shapeshifting pig, another idea derived directly from the legend. The dragon horse in the legend may have given rise to the Earth and Namek dragons. The entire premise of Dragon Ball Z is the same as in the legend: many adventures, many fights, supernatural stuff, dragons, and a giant super-powered glowing-eyed monkey who survives tremendous blasts of fire.

Also, in the Monkey King Legend, the wanderers encounter North, East, South, and West gates. In Dragon Ball Z, heaven is divided into North, East, South, and West sections. A Guardian, such as Kami, controls each section.

Speaking of Giant Monkeys, in Japan, kids see the Giant Monkey as truly GIANT. They see Dragon Ball movies on movie screens rather than television screens. I bet it's really cool to see Dragon Ball Z on a big screen. According to

Danny, another Dragon Ball Z movie will be released on video this summer. We'll see. That'll be great, but not as terrific as seeing the movie in a theater.

I'd like to see a two-hour (or longer) Dragon Ball Z feature film. I've never been to an IMAX theater, one of those giant movie places with three-story-high screens and three-dimensional images and surround-sound. Danny's been to the IMAX in New York City. We have one around here, but neither one of us has been to it yet. Well, we want to see Dragon Ball Z in an IMAX theater! That would be the ultimate. A three-story-high Bubbles the Monkey. A three-story-high Oolong the Pig. Oh, and of course, the three-story-high Goku, Vegeta, Piccolo, etc. All in a huge movie theater with hundreds of other Dragon Ball Z fans.

We'll tell you more about the Dragon Ball Z sagas and episodes later in the book. And Danny will tell you about his favorite episodes, energy blasts, and characters. Right now, however, it's time for a—

Fast Fact Quiz!

The Nameks are based on what animals?

Answer 1: Lizards

Answer 2: Caterpillars and grasshoppers

Answer 3: Snails and slugs

Answer 4: Elephants

3

Are You a Dragon Ball Z Fanatic?

"I liked it when Captain Ginyu got transformed into a frog. A frog in Captain Ginyu's body was hopping around, and Captain Ginyu in a frog's body was hopping around."
—Ed, 11 years old

"I wish my twin brother, Patrick, would transform into a frog."
—Rick, 10 years old

You know you watch too much Dragon Ball Z if . . .

. . . you wear a huge shower cap instead of a pair of shorts and say that you're Fat Majin Buu.

. . . you wear red pajamas and a black sash to school.

. . . you attach a cardboard tube to your rear end and say that it's a tail.

. . . you put dye in your hair to make it blond and stick it up with hair gel so you look like a Super Saiyan.

. . . you toss baseballs into the bathtub to make tidal waves while screaming "Kameha-meha!"

. . . you take a piece of paper, turn it into an eye scouter, and say that everyone's power level is six and your power level is 5 million.

. . . you put underwear over your shirt and tell your friends it's armor.

. . . you name your dog "Bubbles" and then

you teach him how to jump up and down like a monkey and twirl like a top.

. . . you beg your mother to let you sleep in your dog Bubbles' bed because it looks like a Saiyan spacepod.

. . . you get a cat because you want sensu beans.

. . . you use Magic Marker to put dots on your head so you can look like Krillin.

. . . you make your family go on vacations to a swamp, a tornado, and a snoring ogre's castle so you can hunt for dragonballs.

. . . you rip off your shirt in the grocery store and tell the checkout lady that you're Goku.

. . . you eat all the food at the grocery store, and then when the manager says you have to pay for it, you rip off your shirt and claim that you're Goku and you had to eat all the food to save the world.

. . . while screaming "Kaio Ken!", you stuff balloons under your shirt to make you look muscular.

. . . every time you get an answer right on a spelling test, you hop around like a Ginyu Force ballerina.

. . . you hack up your PlayStation, melt some iron on the stove, drip the hot iron on the PlayStation, and tell your mother that you're installing Japanese PlayStation chips so you can play Dragon Ball Z video games.

. . . you roll your black cat into a ball, bounce it on the floor, and shriek that the planet's going to blow up from your Super Saiyan power attack.

. . . you blow grapefruits across the cafeteria, claiming to be Frieza or Nappa.

. . . you eat doughnuts in a forest while trees are falling on your head so you can pretend to be Yajirobe.

. . . you call your mother's car the Nimbus.

. . . you glue a plastic eyeball on your head and say that you're Tien.

. . . you walk down the hall like a robot, muttering, "Button-Dash-Left" and "Button-Energy-Bolt."

. . . you write school reports in Kanji instead of the English language.

Fast Fact Quiz!

Nappa had hair once in:

Answer 1: The Cartoonorama Hour
Answer 2: The Burter TV special
Answer 3: The King Kai film festival in Italy
Answer 4: The Bardock TV special

4

Dragon Ball Z Characters: Good Guys vs. Scum and Filth

"A fine display of dust if such were your intention."
—Raditz to Piccolo when Piccolo shoots some energy at him

It's always about Scum and Filth, isn't it? All the best stories and cartoons are about superhero good guys battling the most vile Scum and Filth in the universe. We expect the good guys to win, and we have faith that they'll always come out on top. But somehow, we always worry that they'll get really hurt this time, that maybe they won't wobble to their feet using their last shred of strength and then beat off those bad guys and save the world once again.

It's exciting, and we can't get enough of it.

How good a story or cartoon is depends on how good the heroes are and how bad the Scum and Filth turn out to be. Are they evenly matched? Or better, are the bad guys a little stronger than the good guys, posing a horrible threat to mankind and all that's good in the world?

We want our good guys to work hard before they win their battles. We want them to pump iron and do situps—Goku does 10,000 situps prior to his fights on the planet Namek. We want them to run millions of miles to build up their already tree-trunk-wide leg muscles. Then we want them to fly so fast they can't be seen. Whatever it takes, we want it, and the more we get, the happier we are.

No doubt about it, Dragon Ball Z delivers.

And we're not talking about *pizza*.

Good Guys

We all know about Goku, Gohan, Krillin, and Piccolo: the main good guys in Dragon Ball Z. We'll tell you about them, of course, but also about some other heroes of Dragon Ball Z and what we think of them.

First, there's *Goku*. He's the main hero. He's the strongest man in the universe, and maybe beyond the universe, into whatever infinity might lie out there. He's a peaceful guy, and he only fights when Earth and the good guys are threatened. In Dragon Ball Z, of course, that means that Goku fights all the time! Earth is constantly being threatened by super-powered morons from outer space. And these bad guys have only one thing in mind: destroy the entire planet.

Goku flies so quickly that bad guys don't see him coming. He shoots energy blasts of all types at bad guys. He obtains powers far beyond 1 million, when he becomes the first guy to become a Super Saiyan in perhaps a thousand years.

Actually, a Super Saiyan is *supposed* to come along every thousand years, but in this case, it's been 3,000 years since the last Super Saiyan existed.

If there's supposed to be only one Super Saiyan born every thousand years, then why are there so many Super Saiyans living at the same time during Dragon Ball Z? We have Goku, Gohan, Vegeta, Trunks, Goten (Goku's second son—we'll get to these guys soon), Gotenks (okay, we'll tell you about another character—Gotenks is the fusion of Trunks and Goten), Vegetto (the fusion of Goku and Vegeta). Read on. You'll find out more about fused characters later, we promise.

For now, the basics: *what's a Super Saiyan?*

A guy with yellow hair and green eyes.

Well, actually, a Super Saiyan is a little more than a guy with yellow hair and green eyes. They're so powerful that it's hard to beat them.

As Danny points out, characters sometimes do beat Super Saiyans: "Remember, Mom, that Goku beat Super Saiyan Vegeta into pulp."

Good point.

Yet Super Saiyans rarely ever lose a battle against someone who isn't a Super Saiyan.

They're surrounded by auras of *pure power*. I was blown away the first time I saw Goku transform into a Super Saiyan. Goku eventually achieves Super Saiyan Three form, and in Dragon Ball GT, he achieves Super Saiyan Five power.

At the beginning of the Dragon Ball Z story, when Raditz comes to Earth from the planet Vegeta, Goku learns the terrible secret of his past. Much to his horror, Goku learns that he was born a Saiyan on Vegeta, and worse, he is Raditz' brother. His Saiyan name is Kakkarot.

Now suppose you're approximately Goku's age and you already have a four-year-old-son. Your name is Joe Shmoe, and you grew up thinking yourself an orphan. In fact, you grew up in some remote and isolated forest, and even more bizarre, you spent your childhood with an ancient martial arts master. You know a giant talking turtle. You zip through the sky on a magic nimbus cloud. You fly.

In short, your life is already pretty weird. So one day, a creep named Raditz shows up and claims that you're a Saiyan, that you're his brother, and that your real name is Kakkarot, which means carrot.

Big deal. After the life you've led as Joe Shmoe, why would you be so surprised by this news? Finding out that you're Kakkarot the Saiyan is mild news compared to learning that your son has a monkey tail, pigs are shapeshifters, and a gigantic Eternal Dragon lives inside your planet.

If anything, Goku should be relieved! His brother could have turned out to be a shapeshifting pig or universe-devouring sea monster! Or Goku could have learned that he was really one cell instead of a whole person, or that his mother was an evil android from the future. Other characters have these problems in Dragon Ball Z. Goku gets off easy.

"Doctor, I have a problem. I married an evil android from the future after a one-celled man ate her and then threw her up." That sums up Krillin's life at the end of the Dragon Ball saga, doesn't it?

Or think about Cell's life story: "Doctor, I have a problem. I'm really one cell, but I eat people and then I get bigger. Sometimes I have to . . . uh, sorry, but I throw up the people, and then . . . I . . . oh, Doctor, you gotta help me!" Wacko sicko guy, that Cell.

Or take another character, Fat Majin Buu. "Doctor, I have a problem. I turn guys into giant candies and then I eat them. I'm really fat because of my bad habit. But I can't seem to help myself! Oh, Doctor, you gotta help me!"

Now compare these problems with Goku's little problem in the beginning of Dragon Ball Z. "Doctor, I have a problem. I just learned that I have a brother, and he's an evil Saiyan." Not too shocking compared to what the doctor just heard from Krillin, Cell, and Fat Buu.

For those of you who haven't seen all these episodes, don't worry, you'll hear more about them in a later chapter. For now, just relax in the knowledge that Goku has a pretty normal life compared to some of his friends. Also, think about all the fun episodes you haven't seen! You have a lot to look forward to in life. Which reminds me . . .

As I'm writing this chapter, I'm missing the all-day 24-hour Dragon Ball Z marathon on the Cartoon Network. There's a two-hour miniseries Garlic Junior show that I'm missing! I am so bummed. But Danny and I are committed to giving you the finest Dragon Ball Z book we can, and that means long, grueling, hard hours of slave labor here at our computer, thinking and writing and plotting and beating our heads against the desk. My fingertips have lost all skin because of the weeks of endless typing. My brain can think of nothing but Goku. I go to the grocery store to get peanut butter for Danny's lunches, and my mouth can't form the words, "peanut butter" and instead my mouth says, "dim sum," as I stare blankly at the grocery lady. She looks at me kind of funny and asks what I mean, and I say, "I don't know, lady, but it has something to do with Yamcha and hot tea."

So don't feel bad, those of you who haven't seen all the episodes. Danny and I are in the same boat. We're missing that great Garlic Junior miniseries *right now*!

Anyway, let me continue to fill you in on the saga, as we know it thus far. As the story goes, the Saiyans sent baby Goku to Earth, figuring he'd leave his Saiyan eyeball spacepod and conquer the world. This happens to make sense to us. When the moon is full, Saiyans become Giant Monkeys who can indeed conquer the world.

Instead of taking over the world, baby Goku bumped his head and forgot the evil Saiyans' plans for him. To this day, he always seems to be in a daze. His face has an almost permanent goofy grin on it. He doesn't seem to have studied much math or science. Don't you wonder why ChiChi fell in love with Goku and married him? She's so insistent that Gohan study constantly, yet her own husband never graduated from kindergarten. It is most peculiar! I think she loves Goku because he's so wonderful, kind, honest, and just . . . well, just plain nice. But she worries about her son, Gohan, growing up to be a martial arts superhuman fighter like his father. It's a dangerous profession.

Some kid: My dad's an accountant. What's your dad do?

You: Oh, nothing much.

Another kid: My dad's a bank manager. Come on, what's your dad do?

You: My dad is The Strongest Man on Earth.

Kid: What kind of job is that?

You: Well, he fights aliens every day and saves the planet from total destruction.

If you had this conversation with other kids at school, they'd probably beat you up on the playground. Or maybe you'd get detention for lying in class.

Teacher: So what did you do over summer vacation?

You: Helped my dad fight dead zombie guys who were trying to destroy the Earth.

Principal: So, Beelzebub Ed (assuming your name is Beelzebub Ed), what did you ever do over Christmas vacation?

You: My dad and I took a spaceship to the planet Namek, where we battled evil aliens who were trying to destroy the universe.

Gohan, of course, is Goku and ChiChi's son. He looks just like a little Goku. He's adorable, thrifty, kind, reverent . . . oh, wait a minute, that's the Boy Scout oath or pledge! But still, everything you can say about a Boy Scout applies to Gohan, as well, and even to Goku, grown up as he is.

In the beginning of Dragon Ball Z, Gohan wails and whines constantly. He's a toddler.

As a toddler, Danny didn't wail and whine much, but of course, he wasn't swept away by the Namek Piccolo to train alone in the wilderness surrounded by wild animals.

If all Danny had to eat for a few days was a couple of apples, he's be starving to death, too. Some dinosaur tail chops would be tasty. Anything would be tasty after several days of starvation. Insect soup would be tasty. Broiled liver and spinach. Cat Chow.

I can't imagine Danny surviving his earliest years without heavy doses of cookies, bananas, and cereal. I wonder what Gohan eats when he's "on the road" constantly, fighting evil aliens to save the world. You never see Gohan eating a bowl of cereal or a cheese sandwich.

So Gohan has good reasons to wail and whine when Piccolo sweeps him away to train in the wilderness. And Piccolo whacks him around a lot, too. I don't like that part. It gives me the creeps.

Gohan turns out to be tenacious—that means he doesn't give up, he's very strong-willed. He turns out to be tougher and stronger than anyone, even Piccolo. Eventually, when Gohan becomes the first Super Saiyan Two, he defeats Cell. Gohan is also the character later known as The Great Saiyan Man. That character fights bad guys with Videl, who is the daughter of a guy named Mr. Satan. Gohan actually marries Videl and has a daughter, Pan.

Here's an interesting fact: In Japan, the voices of Goku and Gohan are done by a woman named Masako Nazawa.

Krillin is Goku's best friend. They once studied martial arts together under Master Roshi. Krillin's special power is a Destructo Disk, which slices objects (or bad guys) in half. He often slices the tops off mountains; by accident, of course—he's really aiming at bad guys. Krillin trembles and moans a lot, but when push comes to shove, he fights with the best of them. He volunteers to go to Namek to help gather the dragon balls. He fights the Saibamen, vegetable-like fighters who grow like weeds.

I think Krillin was bald when he was six years

old, don't you? Yet when he gets old and marries Android 18 (I tell you about It-Her later), he grows a bunch of brown hair.

> "Why do they always have to beat up poor Krillin?"
> —Sarah, age 11

> "Krillin never gives up, and he's a pretty nice guy."
> —Ryan, age nine

Piccolo is the second-strongest guy on Earth. Although he looks like a slug and has green skin, nobody realizes that he's from another planet. As Danny says, "How can they not know he's an alien when he can sit on a cloud and blow up mountains just by thinking about them?"

Danny also points out that Piccolo spits and fumes constantly, and he threatens to destroy Goku with his horrible attacks. But he never does try to destroy Goku, so he's a good guy pretending to be a super-macho bad guy.

Another interesting thing about Piccolo is that he can regenerate lost body parts. That mean he can grow a new arm if he loses one. Various worms can do this in real life. I remember dissecting such a worm in high school, and when I cut it down the middle (as the teacher forced us to do, though I didn't require much forcing—I thought it was pretty cool), it grew a second long body part with a second head. Piccolo reminds me of that worm long ago.

Bulma is another good guy, but she doesn't have an action figure and she never directly fights bad guys. I find Bulma kind of annoying. She's just too mean, and I think Dr. Briefs should have sent her to her room more often when she was a little girl. She is *nasty*. All of the good guys are afraid of her, even Goku. Speaking of which, Bulma was the first human that Goku encountered when he came to Earth in his eyeball spacepod. Bulma grew up to be an expert with all types of technology. This is because her father happens to be the famous Dr. Briefs, founder of the Capsule Corporation (which makes everything on the planet). Her grandfather is Dr. Boxer Shorts, and her grandmother is Dr. Athletic Socks. Her uncle and aunt are Mr. and Mrs. Stained Yellow T-Shirt.

Okay, you caught me. I'm exaggerating. I'm in a nasty Bulma mood tonight. I think I'll eat my keyboard. Grr.

It was at the Capsule Corporation that Bulma learned how to rewire everything from alien devices to spaceships. She can *make* spaceships out of eggshells, telephone wire, and some eyelashes and dustballs. She can build robotic dune buggies in a deserted cave in the middle of a desert on an alien planet. She can take an ordinary toaster and transform it—within one hour—into a flying saucer and then go to Mars.

Bulma is an electronics genius. For some reason, she's madly in love with Yamcha, the (most-of-the-time) dead Hollywood stuntman. Wanting to please this dead stuntman, she's obsessed with glamour and what she looks like.

She constantly yells at everyone. I think she scares Krillin more than when he's confronted by the Saibamen.

Although Bulma's not exactly normal, she has one attribute of normal womanhood. She ends up not being in love with the most-of-the-time dead guy. Instead, she ends up marrying Vegeta. Now, most normal teenage girls would fall in love with Vegeta before batting an eyelash at Yamcha.

(I shouldn't be making so much fun of Yamcha. Who knows? Maybe he's a great bowler.)

Anyway, Bulma does wind up with *The Guy*, Mr. Vegeta Prince himself, Head honcho. Guy with attitude. Maybe the only guy in the universe who can handle Bulma and her horrible temper.

Yamcha is apparently afraid of Bulma (who wouldn't be?). We're never told this is true, but he avoids her throughout Dragon Ball Z, so . . .

Yamcha is like a hired stunt actor in Hollywood. He wants to fight with all the other heroes because, I think, he wants to feel like a hero. He's not one of my favorite characters, so I don't have much to say about him. He doesn't appear often enough in the main battles for me to possess a definite opinion about him one way or the other. He's Bulma's (sort-of) boyfriend, and that's about it in my mind. He also has fork cuts on his cheek. Maybe Bulma sliced up his face during a dinner date. Oh, and he is human—pure human—which is unusual in Dragon Ball Z. Maybe in the time of Dragon Ball Z, all 100 percent humans have fork cuts on their cheeks. Or maybe some of the 100 percent humans have spoon gouges instead.

You can't pay attention to me, by the way, when I'm sitting here, making fun of Yamcha's fork cuts. After all, why listen to me? I'm a grown woman who eats pizza for dinner every night and who talks to stuffed pigs when I think nobody's around.

Tien's claim to fame is that he has three eyeballs. We never find out why he needs the third eyeball or what good it does him, though Dan and I are very curious about this subject. We figure that maybe Tien can see into the future with his third eyeball, or that he can see inside his own brain with it. Who knows? Maybe it's an x-ray vision third eyeball.

ChiChi is Gohan's mother. She was Goku's childhood sweetheart and now is his wife. She worries constantly, and with good reason. If my four-year-old boy was constantly fighting superhero bad guys from outerspace, I'd be plenty worried, too. And if my husband was never home—for years at a time—because he was fighting superhero aliens, well, I'd be a bundle of nerves, too. In fact, ChiChi's husband, Goku, even dies, and she has to worry about whether he'll ever come back to life. Even the wives of policemen and detectives don't have to worry about their dead husbands coming back from the grave! Or worrying about what they're doing as dead guys in the Other Realm.

ChiChi's really funny. Sometimes, she gets really ticked off and whips out a huge machine gun and tries to defend her little home and family from . . . why, from a pack of dead zombie guys in the movie, *The Dead Zone*!

Now, Danny and I lived in the country for a long time. The two of us were all alone in a house in the middle of nowhere. The power went out. We lost all water in the house. We had no lights, no electricity, for days at a time. We had snakes, half-dead pigeons staggering around the yard, pieces of deer hit in the road then tossed on our lawn, we had chipmunks in the attic, we fought off wolves and wolverines and rabid foxes and maniacal sheep and fish people from the lagoon and once, I swore I saw spaceships land in the cornfield behind our house and all the farm trucks head to the top of the field to meet the aliens.

(Believe all that?)

My point (and I actually do have one) is that, no matter how bad Dan and I had it in our house in the middle of nowhere, no matter what we had to fight together, we never had to battle a pack of dead zombie guys.

So, in my humble momlike estimation, ChiChi packs a powerful punch, and I don't mean of the fruit juice type.

The *Ox-King* is ChiChi's father. Back in Dragon Ball (as opposed to Dragon Ball Z), he was a main character when Goku was (stupidly) fighting him. Now, the Ox-King is a minor character, who hangs around with Puar, Oolong, and Master Roshi's turtle, being goofy and saying funny things.

I've heard a lot of rumors about *Master Roshi*. Some kids say he's just a dirty old man. Some kids say he's a mysterious and powerful martial arts master. I think both rumors are right. But I have my own opinion about Master Roshi. Sure, he's the fellow who taught Goku how to do the Kamehameha attack, and sure, he's the fellow who likes toilet jokes too much. But I think the main oddity about Master Roshi is that he wears a giant turtle on his back. Now come on, this is a very weird habit! Kame is the Japanese word for turtle, so not only is Master Roshi attached to a turtle, but he lives in Kami-Turtle House and he teaches a technique that could be called the Turtle Attack. I bet he fell off his bike when he was a little boy and bumped his head really bad. When he woke up, a turtle was crawling past his head, and he became obsessed with turtles starting right then.

Yajirobe is one of Danny's favorite characters. Yajirobe has one interest: food. He's also selfish and lazy. He looks like a caveman with a club. He lies a lot. Sometimes, he saves the day, such as when he cuts off the tail of the Giant Vegeta Monkey. Another interesting tidbit about Yajirobe is that he cannot fly. Almost everyone in Dragon Ball Z flies.

Kami's a grandfatherly alien creature who protects the planet all the time. He lives in a tower that floats above the Earth, and he has a servant named *Mr. Popo*. I always wonder how he chose

Mr. Popo from all the people on Earth to be his servant. After all, Kami's almost like a god, he's The Guardian of the planet, so Popo has a very privileged position. In addition, because Kami created Earth's dragon balls, I sometimes wonder if Popo gets to make wishes whenever he wants, like once a week if he does a really good job baking the bread and greeting the visitors. I mean, is Popo a butler, a maid, a cook, or what? And how much does Kami pay him, to remain up there on the floating tower, all alone without a family, just alone up there with this Kami guy on a tower? I hope Popo's in a labor union, or something.

King Kai lives at the end of Snake Way on a tiny planet. He trains guys to perfect their martial arts fighting . . . if and only if they manage to survive the journey down Snake Way. My math teachers always said, if and only if, as if *if* alone didn't get the point across. I've always thought it was cool to say, if and only if, as if saying, if and only if, made me sound really important and smart. And if a whiff of jiffy skipper flips down a ski lift if and only if . . .

On second thought, it really doesn't make me sound very important and smart, does it?

Danny can sound important and smart. He knows how to spell this word that's 45 letters

long with 19 syllables: pneumonoultramicroscop-
icsilicovolcanoconiosis. He can spell it in three
seconds. I've timed him. It's true. It was a spelling word in Mr. Genthner's fifth grade class. We
have now made Mr. Genthner immortal by put-
ting him in this book, and that feels good. Mr.
Genthner deserves to be immortal. And we can
do that for him *without* collecting dragon balls
from all over the planet.

I suddenly feel very powerful.

I don't quite recall how we moved from King
Kai to Mr. Genthner—

"Is there a resemblance, Dan?"

"No, I didn't think so, I'd remember a green
teacher with catfish tentacles on his face—"

I think it's time to return to King Kai before
I'm the cause of my son flunking out of the fifth
grade.

I must behave myself. I am a grown woman.

King Kai is one of our favorite characters, and
we discuss him a bit more in the next chapter.
He's alone on his tiny planet except for two
friends: Bubbles the monkey, and Gregory the
grasshopper. King Kai teaches Goku the really
hard Kaio Ken fighting technique.

King Yemma is the Gatekeeper of the Upper
and Lower Worlds, which is the nice way of saying that he lets dead guys into Heaven or sends

them to Hell. He happens to send super-powerful good guys such as Goku down Snake Way to King Kai's house. He wants good guys to get excellent martial arts training . . . just in case they return from the dead and can save the planet again.

Goten is Goku's second son and Gohan's brother. Goten is much stronger than either his father or brother, and his best friend is Vegeta's son, *Trunks*.

Trunks appears after the Frieza saga, which we'll tell you about later in this book (if you don't already know about the Frieza saga, that is). Trunks comes from the future, and is Vegeta and Bulma's son. This particular Trunks is also known as *Future Trunks*.

Future Trunks comes back through time into the Dragon Ball Z time period to warn everyone that evil androids are coming to destroy the world. He knows that Goku will die of a heart attack, so he gives Goku some futuristic heart medicine.

Interesting. Why can't I be Future Lois? And at the same time, be Present Lois? And maybe, while I'm Future Lois, Danny can be Present Danny. Then we'll switch, and I'll be Present Lois and he'll be Future Danny. If I'm Future Lois and he's Present Danny, then I'll be like his grandmother, I guess. And if I'm Present Lois and he's Future Danny, then maybe we'll go to college together.

This is too weird.

Let's get back to our story.

Trunks, who is not a swimsuit, is an eight-year-old boy; unless, of course, he's Future Trunks, a teenager. Trunks is very strong and mischievous.

In fact, he's so strong and mischievous that he manages to fuse with his best friend, Goten. Actually, Piccolo teaches them how to perform this feat, and after they fuse, they become *Gotenks*.

And Gotenks can transform into a Super Saiyin Three!

Another weird thing about Gotenks is that he's prematurely balding, yet has extremely long and shaggy blond hair. In fact, all the Super Saiyan guys have long and shaggy hair. I wonder why they don't get haircuts. It must be hard to fight rigorous battles with such long hair. It would get in the way. It would get caught on tree trunks, and the guy wouldn't be able to get loose. Or it would blow all over the guy's face, blinding him during a faster-than-lightspeed punching battle.

Dendee is a little boy on the planet Namek. Dendee has no hair. Poor Dendee lost his family when the evil Frieza destroyed them all. I always feel very sorry for Dendee. He's so cute and small, and he tries so hard to help the good guys and save the world. Dendee joins up with Gohan, Piccolo, and Krillin, and after Guru (the oldest guy, the father of all Nameks, and pretty much the defacto king of Namek) gives Dendee special powers, Dendee saves the good guys from death numerous times.

Oolong is a pig.

Puar is a cat who went to school with Oolong.

They must be mentioned because they're silly. They're always clinging to the good guys or bouncing around Kame House while everyone's looking into Baba's crystal ball.

Oh. *Baba* is Master Roshi's witch sister. When the television blows up, the good guys huddle around Baba's crystal ball for live up-to-the-minute viewing of a horrible battle between Goku and Vegeta.

You would expect *Satan* to be the devil, but he's a good guy. He's in the Cell saga, toward the end of the Dragon Ball Z series.

That's enough about the Good Guys. I'm sick of thinking about the Good Guys. I want to think about Scum and Filth now.

Before I start writing about Scum and Filth, however, I think we all need a break from talking about these characters. We need a brief diversion. Some fun and interesting tidbits, something silly. Let's start with the obvious:

Vegetable Characters in Dragon Ball Z

- Raditz, the radish
- Kakkarot, the carrot
- Vegeta, the vegetable
- Yamcha, the dim sum
- Oolong, the tea
- Puar, the tea
- Gohan, the rice (this one, courtesy of Eric in Scottsville)

Now let's move to some tidbits about characters that aren't so obvious.

Things that Characters Say in Dragon Ball Z Comics

- . . .
- !!!!!!!
- Feh! Feh!

What the Fights Sound Like in Dragon Ball Z Comics

- From Part 2, Comic #2, Pages 20–21:

Doom Dooom Doom Doom Doom Doom
RRmmmm
- From Part 2, Comic #8, Pages 18–21:
Bbbm, Pppaabbbbm, Hssh, Bng, Bbnng,
Kmm, Hwi, Wach, Nng, Shping, Shhh,
Hssh, Vnn

What Gohan Says in the Comics When He's Eating Apples

- Munch
- Shlurp
- Crunch
- Nibble
- Chomp

I am now sufficiently revived to write about Scum and Filth, otherwise known as the *Big Bad Boys of Dragon Ball Z.*

Scum and Filth

Some of our favorite Scum are Vegeta, Frieza, Captain Ginyu, Majin Buu, and Cell. There are others, and we'll touch briefly on them, as well.

At the beginning of Dragon Ball Z, a piece of scum named *Raditz* arrives on Earth, planning to destroy the world. Raditz smirks constantly. His hair hangs to his knees and weighs about 100 pounds. It never sticks to his face or gets in the way when he's beating up Krillin and Goku. Anyway, he comes to Earth because he wants Goku to help him conquer the universe with Vegeta. He kidnaps Gohan, but later, Goku and Piccolo join forces to defeat him.

Along with Raditz, the only known surviving Saiyans are Goku, Nappa, and Vegeta. So there's one Saiyan good guy and three Saiyan bad guys.

Why are there only four Saiyans left? Because the evil *Frieza* destroyed their planet, Vegeta, long ago.

So Frieza is even more evil than Raditz, Nappa, and Vegeta. In fact, Frieza was directly responsible for killing Prince Vegeta's father, King Vegeta. Notice how all Vegetas have the same spellings, at least in this book. As Danny likes to point out, the planet is called Vegita, the Prince is Vegeta, and the King is Vegeta. However, you often see the spellings all mixed up, with most everyone's favorite bad guy being dubbed Vegeta, as well as the planet and the King. So I use the word "Vegeta" for everything that has the sound "Vegeta."

In fact, Frieza sometimes appears as "Freiza," and Oolong as "Ooooooooolong." As the authors, we choose spellings that we're comfortable with (such as Oolong rather than the far more difficult Oooooooooolong), but other people may spell these names differently. Our spellings are the correct ones, of course.

Well, now let's get down and dirty and tell you why we're hooked on these bad guys.

Vegeta is the son of the Saiyan King Vegeta, who as mentioned above, was killed by Frieza. As a boy, Vegeta realized that his power could exceed the super powers possessed by his father. In this regard, Gohan and Vegeta share a similarity: at young ages, both knew that their untamed, raw power was far superior to the power of their fathers. And in each case, their fathers were the most powerful beings on the planet.

Vegeta starts as a very bad guy, kind of a cross between the worst guy in rock and roll, a world wrestling champion, and a snotty bully who beats up kids for fun after school. Over time, he joins forces with Piccolo, Goku, Gohan, and Krillin to battle Frieza. He even ends up marrying Bulma.

When he comes to Earth, Vegeta brings *Nappa* with him, and the two of them destroy everything in sight. The good guys are having enough trouble battling Nappa—even before Vegeta gets involved in the fight. It seems, as is the trend in Dragon Ball Z, that our heroes are going to be wiped out by the bad guys. Goku arrives, however, and shows that his skills may suffice to beat

Nappa. For this reason, Vegeta blows away Nappa.

I talk a lot about Frieza later in this book, as he's one of my favorite characters. Following Raditz and Vegeta, Frieza's the next giant piece of Scum and Filth to show up and try to destroy the universe. Frieza changes over time into increasingly powerful and grotesque-looking forms. At first, he's short and slender, and he looks like a weakling. He doesn't fight anyone, he just flies around in a little spacepod, cackling in a high-pitched voice and issuing threats. After his first transformation, he's taller and has muscles. He grows horns, and magically, armor grows out of nowhere to protect his chest. Then he transforms a third time. His head elongates and a gigantic horn-thing stretches from his skull halfway down his body. Because an entire saga is devoted to Frieza (that means he has to fight in a lot of cartoon episodes), he has to become stronger and more frightening over time, so he transforms a final time. In his most powerful form, he's bald, his body is purple and white, each of his hands has three fingers, and each foot has three toes. This may sound silly, but it looks cool in the cartoons. (If you've seen the Frieza saga, you know what I mean.)

Now we'll move right along and talk about

Captain Ginyu. The entire Ginyu Force really gets on my nerves. Danny thinks they're funny. I think they're nutty. They're Frieza's henchmen, supposedly very powerful and hard to beat. However, they dance like Madonna, and they strike silly cheerleading poses. I suppose that they're funny in an odd sort of way.

Ginyu himself is purple with two horns, and his notable power is that he can shift into somebody else's body, and shift the other person into his body. He doesn't die in Dragon Ball Z. Instead, when Goku tosses a frog into the path of Ginyu's change-bodies beam, Ginyu ends up living inside the frog's body.

Captain Ginyu's big, powerful Force consists of Jaice, Recoome, Guldo, and Burter.

Jaice looks like a heavy-metal rocker from the 1980's. He has puffy hair that flows down his back. He talks with an English cockney accent. He's pretty weak by Dragon Ball Z standards. He throws Fireballs, which have all the power of a pillow fight. But he's devoted to the cause of Bad Guys everywhere, and despite running away when the fight gets rough, he teams up pretty well with Burter in earlier battles.

Recoome is an ad for dental clinics everywhere. He sports short tufts of reddish hair, and of course, he sneers constantly like all the bad guys.

Guldo doesn't last long. He dies quickly, despite the fact that he knows how to freeze time by holding his breath. He's short and squat, with two giant knobs on his head instead of horns.

Burter is blue with a tan brain jutting from his skull. He has great flying speed, but he doesn't last long in battle. Vegeta jumps on his throat and kills him.

One of my favorite characters, *Majin Buu*, is more infantile than a four-year-old kid. I like him because he looks like a giant pink puffball with a huge grin on his face. He turns people into candy and cookies, and then he eats them. Nice guy. When a creep shoots Buu's dog, Buu's head smokes and he turns into Evil Buu. Then Evil Buu turns Buu into a cookie and eats him.

Weird.

Buu has an enormous power level, something like 45 million. One interesting thing about Buu is that when he absorbs somebody else—either by eating them in the form of goodies or wrapping himself around them and literally *absorbing* them—Buu's appearance changes to look like the guy he just absorbed.

The final big piece of Scum and Filth in

Dragon Ball Z is *Cell*, a green-speckled Artificial Human with a tail and black wings. He's created by an evil scientist named Dr. Gero.

Androids 17 and 18 are part of the evil android race of the future. They want to destroy the Earth for fun. Gohan fights Perfect Cell, who kind of throws up Android 18. Eventually Android 18 marries Krillin.

I want a girl just like the girl who married dear old dad. Let's face it, every normal guy wants to grow up and marry a robot who's been thrown up by a bad guy.

Fast Fact Quiz!

What King Kai joke was cut from the censored version of Episode 55?

Answer 1: What vegetable gives you gas when you eat it in the morning? Asparagas!

Answer 2: Mango makes you do the tango.

Answer 3: What vegetable does Gregory the Grasshopper hate the most? Squash.

Answer 4: Are you a cow? Wear a hood and nobody will notice.

5

Who Are *Your* Favorite Characters?

A typical dinner conversation at our house:

"I like Frieza because he's so cool."
—Eric

"Well, you'd expect Freeze-uh to be cool."
—Dan

"Uh-huh. Where's that Rice-a-Roni, Dan?"
—Eric

"My mom burned it."
—Dan

I hate to admit it, but that little dinner conversation actually happened. Dan, Eric, his mom, and I went to the movies and saw *Snow Day*—about kids missing a day of school and having loads of fun due to a blizzard—and then we came back to our house for dinner. I didn't burn the Rice-A-Roni, I soaked it in too much water, then added lots of uncooked rice, and it mushroomed into a gigantic blob of burned Rice-A-Roni. I think that's a more accurate description of what happened.

Anyway, another thing that happened is that Dan had a snow day off from school that week, but I had to work in my half-cubicle, so Dan had to spend the day playing games on my cubemate's computer. So much for snow days and Rice-A-Roni.

But I found out who Eric likes most in Dragon Ball Z: Frieza.

And Danny and I started talking about how

we'd write this chapter. He decided to ask a bunch of his friends about their favorite characters, then summarize all their answers for me. So we created an official questionnaire. Here it is:

1. Who are your favorite good guys? (Examples: Gohan, Goku, Bulma, Master Roshi, King Kai.)

2. What do you like about your favorite good guys? (Examples: King Kai looks like a catfish, cracks lots of jokes, and has a very funny monkey named Bubbles; or Goku always saves everyone, and he never thinks about using his strength to gain personal wealth or power over other people.)

3. Who are your favorite bad guys? (Examples: Vegeta, Frieza.)

4. What do you like about your favorite bad guys?

5. What are your favorite episodes of Dragon Ball Z? (Examples: I like the part where Frieza transforms the second time because he looks creepy and his tongue is really long.)

6. What are some of the funniest things about Dragon Ball Z?

Now, up front, I will tell you that nobody selected Gohan as their favorite good guy, which makes me sad. Gohan is my personal choice for favorite good guy because he's only a little kid and he's adorable, yet he always protects and saves everyone, and well . . . he's just very cute. If Danny were a superhero cartoon-comic book guy, he'd be just like Gohan, only five years older.

I will also tell you that nobody selected Bulma, which doesn't surprise me.

I will also tell you that I like Bubbles a lot, but you'll probably figure that out as you read this book.

Now, most people like Vegeta far more than any other bad guy. I think that's because Vegeta is a bad boy who turns good, he's kind of wicked but there's something very cool about him, as if he's a rock star. I personally prefer Frieza because he's pure evil and it takes forever to get rid of him. When he transforms into the giant-muscled horned thing, he looks really creepy.

Nobody mentioned the Ginyu Force in their list of favorites. Have you ever noticed that they act like cheerleaders or ballerinas? And that they Strike a Pose like Madonna did about ten years ago (probably when you were a baby)?

Finally, I will mention that I'm disappointed

that Oolong the Pig doesn't get a bigger role on Dragon Ball Z. I'd also like to see a giant-sized Oolong action figure.

Now we'll move to the good stuff: Danny's interviews and his own opinions about good guys and bad guys on Dragon Ball Z.

Of the good guys, Eric likes Krillin best, but for no particular reason. However, lots of kids like Krillin because he always does his best against terrible odds, he works really hard all the time, he's very modest, and he's a good friend. Krillin's a nice guy, a hero in his own right.

Another Eric, also 11 years old, likes Goku best "because he always saves the day." His favorite bad guy is Vegeta "because he eventually becomes good."

Robbie, 10, likes Goku, Gohan, Krillin, and Piccolo because all of them are "strong and funny."

Faraz, 10, likes Krillin best "because he's so awesome." He likes Vegeta best "because he is very powerful."

These are just some stray comments, but they're pretty representative of what most kids think about the characters. When asked about their favorite character, good or bad, about one-third of all kids respond Vegeta, and one-third of all kids vote for Goku. Krillin always gets a fair number of votes, though not nearly as many as Goku and Vegeta.

Favorite bad guys? Almost always it's Vegeta, though Nappa weighs in heavily, as does Frieza. I think Nappa gets votes because most people have seen the Nappa cartoons, whereas few people have seen the Satan, Cell, and Buu episodes.

Now let's hear what Danny thinks because he's a real expert when it comes to this stuff.

"Okay, my favorite characters are Goku (Kakkarot), Gohan, Vegeta, and King Kai. What I like best about Goku is that he's very funny; for example, whenever possible, he eats tremendous amounts of food. He also saves the planet a lot, and after he does that, he's usually injured or very hurt. But he doesn't mind, he keeps saving everyone anyway. It's also cool how he becomes a Super Saiyan.

"Gohan is funny, and I like the way he says 'Mr. Piccolo' all the time, and the way he laughs. ChiChi makes him study and makes him wear really weird clothes for a four-year-old kid.

"Vegeta is cool because he was the prince of the Saiyans, or he was the prince before Frieza blew up the planet called Vegeta. He's definitely more polite than Nappa, and he doesn't yell as often as most bad guys. He's very strong like most Saiyans.

"King Kai lives in the Other Dimension, which is neat, and he cracks jokes. Some of his jokes are pretty stupid. For example, 'Do you have pig's feet? Wear shoes and maybe no one will notice.' What does that mean? One of his funnier jokes is, 'When King Yemma sits around the house, he really sits around the house.' Get it? King Yemma's so big he does sit *around* the house."

I agree with Dan about King Kai's jokes. Some are bad, some are great. We also think that King Kai is funny as a straight man. A straight man is the guy who sits around, eating steaks at his picnic table while a monkey and some other guy leap across the table in a mad chase. The steak flips into the air, then back down on the table, and the King Kai straight man just keeps eating as if it never happened.

We also like King Kai because he's so dependable. He cares about everyone, teaches them the ultimate martial arts, and has a very good heart. He's like the perfect grandfather.

Not that Dan's grandfather knew anything about martial arts. But had he known something about martial arts, he probably would have been the world's greatest martial arts champion.

But I'm biased. He was my dad.

Of all the good guys, Danny's favorites are Goku and Piccolo. Goku, because he's the strongest good guy and the biggest hero, and also because he's really cool when he transforms into a Super Saiyan. I agree.

Danny says that "Piccolo has too big of an ego, but it's funny how he talks. In the comic books, he says 'Feh' a lot." As an aside, I also note that, in the comics, the odd phrase "..." (yes, that's it, a few periods) is even more common than "Feh". It seems that "..." means that a character is scared or worried, as in the cartoons where everyone's always quivering and saying something that sounds like this: "... ehhhhh ... eh ..." And maybe "Feh" is what a Dragon Ball Z tough guy says instead of spitting chewing tobacco in the gutter, like tough guys do in old black-and-white movies. I think they spit chewing tobacco, but I'm not really sure. Though they do snarl a lot, just like the Dragon Ball Z tough guys. Though they rarely grunt. I remember one episode in which Frieza was transforming again and he spent approximately fifteen minutes doing nothing but grunting, "Ur uh ur uh" while his muscles expanded, horns popped from his back, his tail grew long enough to challenge the Namek Dragon for length, and so forth.

So who is Danny's favorite bad guy? "Either Raditz (Goku's brother) or Vegeta. Raditz can be funny sometimes. At the very beginning of Dragon Ball Z, when Raditz comes to Earth in his little pod, Piccolo hits him with an energy blast. When Raditz isn't even scratched, he says, 'A fine display of dust, if such were your intention.' That was funny. One of Raditz' favorite moves is when he says, 'Watch the birdie' and then he throws an energy blast at the other guy. I think that's funny, too."

Danny isn't sure why he prefers Vegeta to Frieza. He just does. He also likes Frieza, though: "Some kind of freaky alien who transforms into *very* ugly creatures to power up more.

"Frieza is a loser, a liar, and a dirty scumbag."

Well, that sums up Frieza, don't you think?

Fast Fact Quiz!

Trunks is:

Answer 1: a swimsuit from the future

Answer 2: an oak tree that spawns evil

Answer 3: Majin Buu's personal trainer and dietician

Answer 4: none of the above

6

Danny's Top Ten List

"The Cell Juniors are really nasty pigs. But it's good that they're on the show because that's why Gohan goes Super Saiyan Two. That's one of my top ten favorite things about Dragon Ball Z, when everyone starts going Super Saiyan."
—Danny's sister, Rena

"This is *my* top ten list of favorite things that happen in Dragon Ball Z. You can start each one by thinking to yourself, *I like it when . . .*"

<u>Number 10</u>. . . . Frieza has the dragon balls, he doesn't know the secret words required to use them, and Captain Ginyu says, "Should I do the dance of words?"

Note from Lois: I don't know why Danny finds the above Dragon Ball Z excerpt so funny, but he does. I said, "Danny, are you *sure* that's your tenth favorite thing about Dragon Ball Z?" And he said, "Yes, I don't know why, but everytime I think about Captain Ginyu asking if he should do the dance of words, I crack up."

How about this line?

"You don't hang around with the guy for 100 years without learning a little of his language." (Mr. Popo right before he says the Namek word for *Blast Off!*)

Number 9. . . . Yajirobe eats donuts in Kame's lookout while pine trees are falling on his head.

Number 8. . . . Yajirobe hacks off Vegeta's tail, starts to cower behind a rock and then says, "Okay, whatever happens next is not my problem." Danny thinks this is hilarious because Yajirobe pretends to be courageous but is really such a coward.

Number 7. . . . people call Krillin a Chrome Dome.
    As in: "Don't move, Chrome Dome!" (Bad guys to Krillin in Episode 29, "Friends or Foes?")

Number 6. . . . when Bulma hauls Yamcha around by his ear and screams at him because he wants to date Krillin's girlfriend (and others, too).

Number 5. . . . the Ginyu Force falls off King Kai's planet into a bloody pond.

Number 4. . . . Gohan is eating the apples that Piccolo gave to him, and Gohan makes a face and says, "Eeeeew, sour!" Danny says Gohan looks *so* funny when he makes this face. And Danny adds that it's even funnier in the comics.

Number 3. . . . Nappa says to Gohan, "Don't worry. I'll find a nice place for you on the bottom of my boot."

Number 2. . . . Recoome goes "Whaa" like a ballerina, does some "moves," and attacks.

Number 1. . . . Piccolo shoots an energy blast at Raditz and Raditz says, "A fine display of dust, if such were your intention."

Note from Lois: Yes, that is Daniel's favorite line in all of Dragon Ball Z. "A fine display of dust, if such were your intention."

Fast Fact Quiz!

If only King Kai could survive the 10,000 miles of Snake Way centuries ago, how do all of Goku's friends make the trip so easily?

Answer 1: Snores propel them into the sky, where a tornado whisks them to King Kai's place

Answer 2: Bubbles cushion their feet and help them bounce faster

Answer 3: The cricket comes to their rescue

Answer 4: I don't know!

7

Sagas, Episodes, and Movies

"Lunch is a funny character in the original Dragon Ball show. I like her because she has brown hair except when she sneezes. Then her hair becomes blond and she turns psycho and starts killing people. If she sneezes again, then she becomes brown-haired good Lunch again. So there are good Lunches and bad Lunches, just like in the real world."
—School cafeteria worker

[Okay, we admit it: we made up that quote. No school cafeteria worker on the planet has ever said that to a kid who was complaining about leftover fried haddock-liver slivers.]

This chapter briefly introduces you to the sagas and episodes in the cartoon series. We'll also tell you what we think about some of the movies. Finally, you'll learn about the difference between the cut and uncut episodes.

Cut means censored so you can't see horrible things such as a dribble of purple goo on Piccolo's chin. Uncut means you get the pure Japanese version with the goo on Piccolo's chin, which could scare you sufficiently that you never recover. I quivered all night, thinking of that goo. I had terrible nightmares. I still see goo everywhere I go: on subway windows, in my half-cube at work, in the eyes of my boss, on all my fingers.

Actually, the uncut stuff isn't particularly worth censoring. Certainly not in the cartoons. Sometimes, in the uncut comics, Piccolo screams a bad word, but nothing even close to what kids scream on school buses and in the lunch room

or on the playground. He might scream, "Feh!
Feh!" followed by a bad word that sounds the
same as what beavers build with logs.

Well, you almost know all the differences between cut and uncut now, so we might as well
tell you the rest of it. Actually, other than some
goo and a bad word after some "Feh! Feh!"
screams, the only other thing in the uncut episodes is what the video box covers call brief nudity. Danny was particularly shocked by this
claim. The brief nudity consists of the Giant
Monkey's all-fur body, Goku and Gohan shown
from the waist up while bathing in a big barrel,
and once or twice Gohan's rear end, which looks
microscopic falling out of the sky as he returns
to human form from giant ape form. That's about
all we found.

We promised to tell you about the sagas, episodes, and movies in this chapter, and also about
the difference between cut and uncut episodes.
Since we started by talking about cut versus uncut episodes, it only makes sense that we continue to work our way backward.

So we'll talk about the movies next.

By the way, never perform this magnificent
writing feat in school. If you introduce three sub-
jects and then talk about them in reverse order,

your English teacher will flunk you, and I will get in trouble for teaching you how *not* to write a book.

On the other hand, if you can write a backward book in elementary school or junior high, then you're pretty darned smart, and you can say "Feh! Feh!" (but not the bad word that Piccolo screams) to anyone who claims you're not supposed to write topics in backward order.

If you dare to scream, "Feh! Feh!", they'll flunk you, so you'd better not take my advice on that, either.

Okay. The movies, as I promised:

I've only seen a few. My favorite is *The World's Strongest*, starring the evil Dr. Wheelo. In this film, the dragon balls bring evil Dr. Wheelo back to life. Wheelo wants to take over the world by combining his disembodied yet brilliant brain with the body of the world's strongest man. The movie ends when "Dr. Wheelo tries to blow up Earth, but Goku hits him with a spirit bomb and that's the end." That's how Danny puts it.

Another Dragon Ball movie is called *Tree of Might*. In this one, Goku and his companions fight pirates who want to grow trees that devour Earth's energy and destroy the planet. The trees store the energy in their fruit, and anyone who eats the fruit becomes extremely strong.

Danny and I also saw the movie, *The Dead Zone*, in which dead guys wander all over the planet under the guidance of the evil Garlic Junior. It's pretty funny when Gohan comes out of a clock and says, "Wahoo." It's also silly that the movie has bad guys called the Spice Boys: Gingerbread, Tutti, Fruiti, and Macaroni. As they attack Goku, each Spice Boy yells his own name. Here's what Danny has to say about the movie:

"Goku goes after Garlic Junior, but he can't beat him. Garlic Junior creates a black hole called the Dead Zone that sucks everyone into oblivion. Gohan starts to get so mad that he hits Garlic Junior into the Dead Zone. Garlic Junior comes back in episodes 95 through 102."

Overall, it's hard to say much about any of the movies, as they have little to do with the sagas. If you're a big Dragon Ball Z fan, however, then you should see as many of the films as possible. They're fun diversions from the main thread of the series.

But now let's move to the meaty stuff, the stuff that really matters: the cartoon shows!

We'll start our discussion of the cartoon episodes with the original series, Dragon Ball, then dive right into Dragon Ball Z itself.

In the Dragon Ball series, we first learn about the Eternal Dragon, who appears when someone gathers the seven dragon balls from all over the Earth and then utters some magic phrases. The Eternal Dragon then grants the person any one wish. Ten thousand angel food cakes, 45 quadrillion tubs of chocolate marshmallow ice cream—

Sorry, those would be some of my wishes . . .

More likely, Dragon Ball characters ask the Dragon for eternal life, to bring someone back from the dead, or maybe in the case of Bulma, for lots of boyfriends.

Next in the original Dragon Ball series, Bulma as a little girl comes across Goku in the wilderness. As you might predict, Bulma's irritated by Goku even when they're both little. Bulma's always irritated by everyone. The two of them save a turtle and meet the turtle's friend, who of course is Master Roshi.

Danny points out that it's Master Roshi who gives Goku the flying nimbus cloud that only pure-hearted people can fly. I think it's odd that Goku's the only pure-hearted person in the world; after all, I don't remember seeing anyone else ever ride the nimbus cloud.

Also, I must point out that Goku and Bulma meet a shape-changing monster, who turns out to be the little pig, Oolong. My Oolong mini-action figure sits on a special blue pottery tray that Danny's sister made for me when she was in the fourth grade. Oolong occupies the center position on the top of a beautiful stand by my bed. I'm very fond of Oolong, and that's why it's funny to me that a shape-changing monster is really a silly, little pig.

At this point, in the original Dragon Ball series, Goku, Bulma, and Oolong meet Yamcha and Puar, as well as ChiChi and the Ox-King. Well, I'd tell you more but you'll just have to watch the shows.

To make a long story short, they find the seven dragon balls and finally are ready to request their one wish. But lo and behold, terrible Oolong steps in and makes a wish, and that's that, the dragon balls are scattered again all over the planet.

That pretty much sums up Dragon Ball.

The next series, Dragon Ball Z, has four main sagas. A saga is a long adventure story. In Dragon Ball Z, they're called the Raditz (or Saiyan) Saga, Frieza Saga, Cell Saga, and Buu Saga.

Danny and I decided to tell you about our favorite moments in the series in the next chapter. We figured you'd be better off getting a brief idea of what we think about the sagas in this chapter, just to get you warmed up for the next chapter, where we go hog wild.

Raditz Saga

This saga begins with the first episode of Dragon Ball Z. Goku learns that he's a Saiyan, the brother of Raditz, who wants Goku to join the remaining Saiyans in destroying the universe and killing everything in sight.

I can't imagine why anyone, especially the hero of the planet, would want to join a thug in destroying the universe and killing everything in sight. Why would Goku ever consider such an invitation? It's not as if his brother's inviting him to a family reunion, where they're going to have cake and ice cream, and maybe laugh at old family jokes and open some presents. I mean, the guy's asking Goku to blow up the planet! And if that's not enough, along comes Nappa, another creep, not exactly a thrilling enticement to join forces with Raditz. And then, talk about really bad luck, Goku has to meet Vegeta, who isn't exactly friendly.

Goku, whose Saiyan name is Kakkarot, and Nappa, Vegeta, and Raditz are the only living Saiyans. Some evil guy named Frieza destroyed their home planet, Vegeta.

Anyway, a big fight erupts in the Raditz Saga and Goku dies. Piccolo trains Gohan to fight the evil Saiyans who are returning to Earth in one year.

Vegeta Saga

Krillin, Chiaotzu, Tien, and Yamcha go to the floating palace in the sky. Kami, the Namek king of Earth, and his sidekick, Mr. Popo, train everyone for the big fight.

Goku, in the meantime, makes his way down Snake Way to King Kai's planet. Danny and I laughed a lot while watching these adventures. Especially when Goku falls off Snake Way into the Home for Infinite Losers and when Goku eats a lot of food at some princess's palace.

Anyway, Goku trains in martial arts techniques by chasing Bubbles, the monkey, and trying to whack Gregory, the Grasshopper, with a hammer. We watched these episodes repeatedly, laughing every time. Eventually, after eighty-eight days of training, Goku is wished back to life by his friends on Earth. I wish I could train for eighty-eight days with Bubbles, the monkey, and then return to Earth. That'd be a great vacation!

Goku returns, alive again, and defeats Nappa. But not until he fights the Saibamen, which are vegetablelike killers that pop out of the ground. Gohan and Krillin return to the Kame House, leaving Goku alone to fight Vegeta.

As the Vegeta saga closes, the good guys are in bad shape: either dead or badly hurt. They cannot summon the Eternal Dragon for help.

Frieza Saga

After Frieza dies, his father puts him back together; kind of like, Humpty Dumpty sat on the wall, Humpty Dumpty had a great fall, all the king's horses and all the king's men couldn't put Humpty Dumpty together again; except Frieza is put back together again. Frieza returns to seek his revenge on Earth. Frieza's father is called Cold.

Because all the good guys are in really bad shape after fighting Vegeta, they need some dragon balls to bring people back to life. But there's a big hitch: they cannot use Earth's dragon balls. Here's why:

Kami's and Piccolo's dad was the same guy. But this guy split up one day; and one half of him became Piccolo-Daimaou, who was Piccolo's dad, while the other half remained just plain old Kami. Now Piccolo-Daimaou had a boy, conveniently named Piccolo. So you see, Piccolo and Kami are blood relations. Dan and I aren't sure exactly what relationship they share, however. Is Kami really Piccolo's father? No, because that was Piccolo-Daimaou. Yet Kami was half of the guy who turned into Piccolo-Daimaou. So maybe Kami is Piccolo's half-father, whatever that means. All Dragon Ball Z fans know that if Piccolo dies, then Kami dies, as well. This fact implies that the two of them are something more than half-father and son. It implies that they literally *share* blood; that they are the same person somehow...yet they clearly aren't the same person. It's a point of confusion in the show.

Another aspect to all of this Kami-Piccolo relationship stuff is that, if Kami dies, then the dragon balls disappear. We're told that the dragon balls disappear because Kami created them.

Now this is a curious and puzzling fact. Here I sit, writing this book so Dragon Ball Z fans like you can read it, write to me, and either disagree with what I'm saying or agree with it. But let's suppose that I die (I sure hope not, but this is all hypothetical and for the sake of argument). Okay, so I'm dead and buried. You're still sitting in your comfy armchair, reading this book, or in the bathroom or on your bed, or whatever—the point is the book doesn't *die* just because I die.

So why do the dragon balls vanish if something horrible happens to Kami?

Okay, well anyway, Piccolo and Kami are not exactly in great shape, so there are no dragon balls for anyone to use on Earth. However, the good guys *can* go to Namek, which is Piccolo's home world, and get more dragon balls there. That's exactly what they do in the Frieza saga: go to Namek.

Mr. Popo teaches Bulma how to fly the ship that originally brought Piccolo to Earth a long time ago. Goku can't make the trip. He's in the hospital, wrapped like a mummy in bandages. ChiChi throws a huge fit, but she can't stop Gohan from heading off to Namek with Bulma and Krillin to seek dragon balls. As I explain in the next chapter, this entire adventure is one of my favorite parts of Dragon Ball Z. I love the episodes in which the good guys are seeking the Namek dragon balls.

Enter Vegeta again. He recovers from the near-death he survived during the Vegeta saga. He learns that Frieza is after the Namek dragon balls. Being Vegeta, he's furious—nobody can beat him at anything! Not ever!—and Vegeta zooms off to Namek to beat Frieza in the big search for dragon balls.

Enter Frieza. With his two nasty henchmen, Zarbon and Dodoria, Frieza's collecting dragon balls by roaming across the Namek countryside, killing everyone in sight and screaming that they gotta have dragon balls. Nice, huh?

It's Dodoria who attacks Dendee, the little Namek boy who later joins forces with the heroes and even takes over Kami's position. Gohan and Krillin rescue Dendee from Dodoria, but it's Vegeta who kills Dodoria.

Like I said, the Frieza saga is one of my favorites, so I get a little carried away when I think about it, especially the way Vegeta keeps coming back for more.

Zarbon beats up Vegeta pretty badly, and Vegeta has to recover again, this time to be tried for treason by Frieza. However, Vegeta escapes from Frieza's recovery chamber and steals all of the dragon balls that Frieza has collected.

Frieza tells Zarbon to kill Vegeta and get the dragon balls back. He also summons Captain Ginyu and his Force.

Now begins some of the silliest stuff in Dragon Ball Z: the antics and dancing of the Ginyu Force. Danny thinks these guys are really funny. I can barely stomach watching them twirl and pose. So Danny laughs hysterically, while I sit there, grimacing and waiting for Frieza to turn into a real monster and bump them all off. That's how we watch the Ginyu Force.

There's a huge fight between Vegeta and Zarbon, and of course, Vegeta finally wins. At this point, Vegeta has seven dragon balls, and he figures that's all he needs to summon the Eternal Dragon. He has one that he took from Krillin, one that he hid in a lake, and five that he swiped from Frieza.

As everyone's arguing about which person should become immortal, the Ginyu Force arrives, and Gohan, Krillin, and Vegeta realize that they're in for another huge battle. The Ginyu guys have never lost a fight, which is hard to believe, since they act like fools and it's apparently easy for the good guys to defeat them.

There's one really excellent scene with the Ginyu Force. Five dragon balls are on the ground. Krillin's holding a dragon ball, and Vegeta's holding another one. Vegeta throws his dragon ball into the air, and Burter uses his super fast flying to race toward the horizon and catch the dragon ball. Then Guldo freezes time and steals Krillin's dragon ball from his hand. Nobody can see this happen because time has frozen. That's the part that we think is pretty cool. When the dragon ball disappears, Gohan and Krillin become very frightened, but then they're always quivering, groaning, and grunting with fear. Oh, and they sweat from fear a lot, too.

Anyway, Captain Ginyu heads off to deliver the dragon balls to Frieza. A huge battle takes place between the Ginyu Force and Krillin, Gohan, and Vegeta. Once again, Guldo uses his freeze technique, and once again, it's a lot of fun to watch. Krillin and Gohan are frozen in place, suspended in the sky. With the good guys just hanging there, incapable of moving, Guldo has open season on both of them, and he just beats them up a bunch, then grabs a tree, which he plans to use as a spear. This part is very scary. Everyone's frozen, and it seems that all is lost. The excitement is almost unbearable.

But Vegeta saves everyone again. For a bad guy, Vegeta sure saves everyone an awful lot.

The battles go on and on. All is hopeless again, but Goku shows up with sensu beans and heals his friends, including Vegeta, who saved Krillin and Gohan.

Fast-forward. More battles. Jaice uses his Crusher Ball. Guru releases Dendee's super powers. Captain Ginyu uses his Change Body attack and shifts into Goku's body, with Goku shifting into Ginyu's body.

Frieza kills Vegeta. Huge fights continue, this time between Goku and Frieza. Because Frieza kills Krillin, Goku gets really ticked off and turns into a Super Saiyan.

Frieza's father, King Cold, and his crew show up. Frieza commands all the bad guys to kill everyone on Earth.

By now, all the people on Earth should be used to alien bad guys trying to destroy everyone and everything. One battle after another. But everyone gets really scared again. The bad guys are about ready to kill everyone in the world, but suddenly, they just fall to pieces—literally, they fall to pieces: they get all chopped up somehow and drop to the ground.

Enter Trunks. He's wearing a Capsule Corporation jacket. He has purple hair. He's very cool. He has chopped up all the bad guys, bam bam, in one quick blast, and he casually shows up as if to say, "Hey, folks, I've just saved the entire world, and how are you doing?"

More battles, each one more dizzying and exciting than the last one, and Trunks finishes off both Frieza and King Cold. At this point, Danny and I are figuring that Trunks is going to turn out to be one major heavyweight dude. And we're not mistaken. He seems more powerful than Goku and Vegeta put together.

So much for the bad guys, at least for now.

Trunks makes a small capsule turn into a refrigerator (all capsules made by the Capsule Corporation transform into whatever we seem to want at any given time), and gives everyone some soda. He announces that he's from the future, when everyone on Earth will die from the attacks of evil androids. He explains that Goku dies of heart disease in this future time, and that he, Trunks, has returned to give Goku the necessary medicine to cure the upcoming heart condition.

Danny and I are awestruck. Not only is Trunks able to save the world from Frieza and King Cold, he can save Goku's life using some special heart attack doctor techniques! This is almost too much!

Now, if you were Goku, hearing all this rot, wouldn't you freak out? Well, that's exactly what Goku does: he freaks. It's awfully bizarre, even for a guy who started life as a monkey-tail alien, to learn that some kid is returning from the future, and that this kid happens to be the son of *Vegeta and Bulma!*

At this point, during the Frieza saga, nobody would think that Vegeta and Bulma are destined to get married and have a child. But whatever, Goku gets his futuristic heart medicine, and then Trunks hops into a time machine and disappears.

Whew. A lot happens in the Frieza saga, even

when we just think about some of the highlights. That's why I think that the Frieza saga is the best one in the series.

Cell Saga

Another great adventure in Dragon Ball Z is the one known as the Cell Saga. This saga combines all sorts of standard science fiction elements. We get androids, biological freaks, and evil scientists in rotting, weirdo laboratories—don't you love that word, laboratory? It sounds very exotic to me. We also get vile creatures who eat everyone in sight, crazy lunatics who grow body parts and brains in vats, and bubbling, sickening messes in test tubes. I love this stuff.

As the saga opens, an evil scientist named Dr. Gero creates Android 19, hoping to destroy Goku. When Dr. Gero asks Android 19 to make Gero into a robot, too, the android complies, and so Dr. Gero turns into Android 20.

While Vegeta's fighting Android 19, he turns into a Super Saiyan and destroys the android. Dr. Gero is also destroyed. However, as in many science fiction stories, Dr. Gero has preprogrammed himself to repair all self-damage, so he isn't really destroyed; his preprogrammed routines kick in and he repairs himself.

Android 20 (Gero) feverishly works to create

a superior android that can withstand destruction, then works on developing a better android model. Android 17 and Android 18 show up and kill Dr. Gero.

So Gero dies *again*.

Sort of.

Dr. Gero was in the process of creating Android 21, who is still simmering in half-concoction mode in a test tube. So Dr. Gero gets some revenge. He/she/it commands Android 21 to destroy the androids who killed him.

Before being defeated, Cell activates a mechanism that ensures the destruction of Earth (of course) should he die. Goku teleports Cell from the planet onto King Kai's planet, where Cell blows up.

Unfortunately, this unselfish and very heroic act means that Goku, King Kai, Bubbles, and Gregory all die along with the evil Cell.

True to Dragon Ball Z nature, a fireball flies out of nowhere and kills Trunks, and voilà, Cell returns. Apparently, when Cell blew up on King Kai's planet, one brain cell survived. This one cell multiplied, and as the cells continued to multiply, the entire evil Cell reformed and came back to life.

More battles. Eventually, Gohan throws a Kamehameha that destroys Cell.

Some guy named Mr. Satan tells reporters that he saved the world from Cell. This is similar to a much earlier episodes in which Yajirobe told reporters that he was the hero of Earth back when Goku and Gohan were beginning to fight the Saiyans.

Goku's dead again, and Krillin's in love with Android 18. End of the Cell saga, and we move to the final one.

Buu Saga

The Buu Saga is even better than the Cell Saga. Now I'm a science fiction writer who specializes in what I call Weird Wired Flesh Blobs. For some reason, I am greatly amused by concocting adventures for creatures who are part computer/machine and part biological/flesh. Naturally, I enjoyed all of Cell's permutations—that means, changes in his shape and form—how he was part android and part person, and then how he mutated into pure biological/flesh form.

However, even for a serious Weird Wired Flesh Blobs person such as myself, Buu beats Cell for sheer entertainment value. I figure they just couldn't come up with anything better after they created Buu, so they had to end the entire Dragon Ball Z series with the Buu Saga.

As this saga begins, all the good guys are

training to become better fighters. Gohan, now a teenager, is dating Mr. Satan's daughter.

Gohan achieves the status of Great Saiyan-Man and attends a martial arts tournament. He turns into his Super Saiyan form and everyone realizes that the Great Saiyan-Man is really Gohan.

Two guys with names that sound like Spopoblitch and Yamuu arrive from nowhere, and they suck up all of Gohan's energy and then stick the energy into a lamp. This lamp revives the evil Buu.

As with all bad guys on Dragon Ball Z, the goal is to destroy all life. And as with all sagas, the Buu saga has lots of battles. In one, Vegeta becomes a bad guy's slave and this is when his forehead is marked with a giant M (for Majin Vegeta). It's the Vegeta M slave's energy that's used to bring Majin Buu back to life.

More martial arts training so the good guys can become better fighters. Goten and Trunks learn how to fuse and they become the much-stronger Gotenks.

Fast-forward again. Buu splits into a good Buu and an evil Buu. The evil Buu turns the good one into a cookie and eats him. Gotenks transforms and achieves Super Saiyan Level Three, but evil Buu eats him anyway.

Then Buu eats Piccolo.

Then Buu eats Gohan.

Then Buu eats pickles.

Then Buu eats salami and clam chowder.

Then Buu eats an entire city, as well as an adjacent country.

Actually, I'm kidding. Buu does eat Piccolo and Gohan, and I bet he wants to eat pickles, salami, clam chowder, an entire city, and an adjacent country, but he controls himself. Maybe he's saving what's left of his gigantic appetite for desert: Krillin with Chocolate Sauce, or Fused Gotenks a la King.

Yeah, here's a pretend menu at the famous Buu's Palace Restaurant:

Entrees: Baked Kami Compote
    Sizzling Swordfish with Dendee Beans
Dessert: Thousands of Cream-and-Bulma-
    Filled Doughnuts, each the Size of the
    Universe

So this guy's eating everyone, and in the meantime, Goku happens to be dead and wears a halo. He has earrings that enable him to fuse with somebody else, with the fused result being super SUPER strong. Being dead, Goku teleports into the battle anyway to fight evil Buu.

Vegeta also happens to be dead, but the Judge of Death sends him into the battle to help Goku fight evil Buu.

Goku wears one of the fusion earrings, Vegeta wears the other, and the two become the great Vegetto.

When evil Buu eats him, Vegetto transforms back into Goku and Vegeta. Of course, they're living inside of Buu's body (remember, Buu *ate* Vegetto!).

My head's beginning to spin. Hang in there. Eventually, everyone escapes from the insides of evil Buu's body.

Inside Buu's body, Goku and Vegeta have a welcome-home party with Trunks, Gohan, and Piccolo. They all leave Buu by escaping through a skin pore.

Poof. They pop back into normal human-Saiyan shape and size. Complete with clothing.

More battles. And finally, everyone raises their hands, Goku gathers all that good spirit energy, and Goku blows away Buu and the world is finally saved.

An odd thing here is that nobody on Earth believes that the world's about to end (again). This is peculiar because the good guys have already saved the world about a trillion times from evil aliens with super powers. It takes Mr. Satan's influence to convince everyone to help by raising their hands so Goku can concoct that huge spirit ball to save the planet from Buu.

I will mention only one more thing about the Buu saga, where the Dragon Ball Z series ends. Good Buu wakes up and joins the heroes, but there are no bad guys left to fight. True to his nature, Goku longs for more battles. So he wishes for evil Buu to come back to life. He gets his wish, sort of . . . as evil Buu comes back as Ubuu, no longer evil and requiring massive amounts of martial arts training to put up a good (although not real) fight.

So Goku gets his wish—martial arts fighting forever—but the difference is that, this time, there's no real threat and no real bad guys, and finally . . .

The world lives in peace.

Fast Fact Quiz!

What is the name of Piccolo's father?

Answer 1: Piccolo-Pickle
Answer 2: Piccolo-Flute
Answer 3: Piccolo-Daimaou
Answer 4: Piccolo-Popo

8

Our Favorite Funny Parts of Dragon Ball Z Episodes

"If you could be inside the Room of Spirit and Time for your whole life, you wouldn't need the Eternal Dragon because you'd be living forever. I mean, for each year that you're in the Room of Spirit and Time, it equals one complete real day, so one real week of time equals seven years in the Room, one month of real time equals approximately 30 years, and 365 days (a year) in real time equals 365 years in the Room. Say you were in the Room for ten real years. That would be like living for 3,650 years. The only problem would be the boredom. Who would want to be in a room alone for 3,650 years with nothing to do?"

—Lois, coauthor of this book

Here we're going to whip through some of our favorite episodes, tell you why we think they're great, and fill you in on some of our favorite moments. These are the things that made us laugh while we watched the shows, the things that we remembered long after the shows were over. We confine ourselves to the shows that you can watch in the United States and England. If you have favorite stuff from these or other episodes, let us know!

Episode 5: "Gohan's Metamorphosis."

Gohan says, "I'm ready, Mr. Piccolo. What do I have to do first for the training?"

Piccolo says, "Just live."

Danny thinks this is funny because it will be very tough for Gohan to survive as a preschooler in a dinosaur-infested wilderness, alone, without food, clothing, or shelter.

Episode 6: "Gohan Makes a Friend." Lots of funny stuff in this episode, such as:

Goku says, "I'm tired. If I was any more whipped, I'd be butter."

Gohan puts bee sting ointment on a dinosaur after pulling out a tree branch (a splinter) from it. The dinosaur licks him. Only two-legged dinosaurs eat people. This dinosaur has four legs.

Gohan eats dinosaur tail chops for breakfast.

At this point, we digress slightly and tell you about two of our favorite Dragon Ball Z comics. You have to read all the comic books, by the way, backward. You open the comic backward, and then you read the bubbles (where the text is put) backward, too.

Comic #6 corresponds to the episode in which Piccolo starts training Gohan. Dan and I laughed a lot when we read this issue.

On page 11, when King Yemma screams "Shut Up!" he looks hysterically funny.

On page 19, Piccolo is really mean when he says to the wailing Gohan, "Silence . . . or I'll slit your throat!" In the English cartoons, Piccolo isn't as violent or nasty as he is in the comics.

On page 28, Gohan says that he doesn't want to be a fighter; rather, he wants to be a great scholar. Danny comments that Gohan never says this in the cartoons.

In Comic #7, we both liked page 14, in which Gohan is eating the sour apple (one of Danny's top ten favorite things about Dragon Ball Z) because the pictures of Gohan are funny and he says stuff like "Munch Shlurp Crunch Nibble Chomp."

Meanwhile, Piccolo watches from afar, muttering, "Cursed brat. Is there no end to it?"

Episodes 23 and 24 Danny especially likes these two episodes. Here's what Danny says:

"When Vegeta is about to blow up the Earth with his Garick Gun, Goku uses the Kamehameha blast to hold off Vegeta's Garick Gun. He also uses the Kaio Ken times four, and Vegeta is hit by it. But Vegeta comes back.

"My favorite saga is the Saiyan Saga, otherwise known as the Vegeta Saga. I like the parts when Piccolo kills Raditz and when Gohan smashes Vegeta. I think that Nappa is a bit annoying when he's screaming about beating everybody, and then Goku takes him down with a couple of hits and Vegeta destroys him."

Episodes 25 and 26. "Stop Vegeta Now!," which is episode 25, is another of Danny's favorite episodes. (He *does* like the Saiyan-Vegeta Saga a lot.) According to Danny, "It's cool when Krillin throws the spirit bomb at Vegeta. Gohan bounces it back, and its hits Vegeta.

"Also, I like the next episode, when Gohan transforms into a giant ape and starts attacking Vegeta. Then Vegeta cuts off Gohan's tail, and Gohan turns back into his human form. But Gohan-as-ape has already jumped Vegeta and falls on top of him. Vegeta is forced to retreat to his pod."

Episode 27 "You don't hang around with the guy for one hundred years without learning a little of his language," states Mr. Popo right before he says the Namek word for *Blast Off!*

Episode 28 This is a really funny episode. Bulma, Krillin, and Gohan take off in a spaceship to seek the planet Namek. Goku is laid up in the hospital.

ChiChi packs Gohan's bowling ball, blow dryer, cookies, and other odd items, for his trip to Namek.

Gohan says, "Mom, put some gel on my head."

Then we switch to Goku in an all-body

mummy bandage, working out in the hospital doing situps and exercises. This episode is funny from start to finish.

Episode 32 is also funny. In "Touchdown on Namek," bad guy monsters Brain Drain the good guys and find out about their spaceship. But as they try to open the ship door, the bad guys yell, "Cheeseburger" instead of "Piccolo."

Episode 33. "Face-off on Namek."

Frieza says, "There are three things I really hate—cowards, bad haircuts, and military insurrection. Our friend Vegeta possesses all three of these." Ha!

Episode 34. Vegeta has a receding hairline. I wonder why Krillin's hat says, "Kulilin." The bad guys want to kill everyone on a planet, so they can sell the stripped planet to their clients, The Planet Trade.

Episode 35. "The Nameks vs. Frieza."

Goku does 10,000 situps. Frieza now has four dragon balls. Frieza has horns. I note here that all bad guys have horns on Dragon Ball Z. Both

Frieza and Vegeta want the dragon balls so they can ask the Eternal Dragon for eternal life. Meanwhile, on the huge spaceship made for him by Bulma's father at Capsule Corporation, Goku does 7,000 more situps and has visions of food. "I'm so hungry!"

Episode 36. "Escape from Dodoria" (who is the big fat pink monster who works for Frieza).

Frieza sounds like the wicked witch of the west. Danny says his chorus teacher sounds like Frieza. Gohan saves Dendee from Dodoria. Krillin grabs Dendee, then the three of them fly away. Dodoria follows them.

Krillin says to Dodoria, "Overgrown sweat gland!"

Episode 37. "Secrets Revealed."

Danny loves it when Dodoria says to Vegeta, "Vegetable-head!"

I, on the other hand, love it when Dodoria heaves heat lasers at Vegeta, who says, "Nice try, Dodo Brain."

Episode 41. "The Eldest Namek."

The eldest Namek, Mr. Guru, is huge. Mr. Guru's voice sounds like Alfred Hitchcock. Do you know who Alfred Hitchcock was? He was an old-time guy who produced popular weird-mystery shows and who compiled similar anthologies of short stories. One of my favorite books in junior high was a scary book compiled by Alfred Hitchcock.

In this episode, Bulma is more worried about her hair than bad guys killing everyone. While toying with her hair, she says, "Would you look at these split ends?"

Episode 47. "Scramble for the Dragon balls!"

One of Frieza's bad guys sounds like a New York City cabdriver, or rather, a thug from a 1930's gangster movie. The other bad guy, a dog-monster, calls Bulma, "Toots." Why do all the alien bad guys sound like old Hollywood movie bad guys?

Frieza says, "The entire universe will know the name of Frieza."

Episode 48. "Arrival of the Ginyu Force."

King Kai says that the Ginyu Force is Frieza's personal army. They have power levels of at least 25,000. Mr. Guru's chair has horns. Ginyu has two horns. Everyone always has horns on Dragon Ball Z.

Episode 51. "No Refuge from Recoome."

After slamming Vegeta into the ground, Recoome says to Vegeta, "I just love picking vegetables out of my garden."

But then Vegeta energy-blasts Recoome's face. It takes away part of Recoome's goofy red hair. As Dan says, "Recoome is a fashion model or ballerina." Recoome suddenly has *more* teeth after lots of fighting. Weird.

Episode 53. "Goku . . . Super Saiyan?"

Captain Ginyu forces his men to Strike a Pose. This is like watching Madonna. Goku reads Krillin's mind. Goku gives Krillin and Vegeta sensu beans.

Vegeta says, "After 3,000 years, another Super Saiyan emerges! Kakkarot!"

A very exciting episode!

Episode 54. "Ginyu Assault."

The cover of the video calls this one "Burter and Jaice," though the actual video calls the show, "Ginyu Assault."

Captain Ginyu tells Jaice he must strike a pose to show new recruits what being a Ginyu Force member is all about. The recruits bury the dragon balls. Captain Ginyu and Jaice do a cheerleader dance while chanting, "We are the Ginyu Force," and then they Strike a Pose.

Episode 55. "Incredible Force."

Captain Ginyu guesses that Goku is a "mutant", and could have a power level of 60,000. Goku and Vegeta team up to fight Captain Ginyu and Jaice. But Vegeta runs away before the fight begins.

And now we come to the *Big Turning Point Show*:

Episode 56. "Frieza Approaches."

An absolutely superb episode, one of our top few favorites.

Goku reaches a power level of 110,000, and is going up now to 117,000. Captain Ginyu's maximum is 120,000. Goku reaches 140,000, then 150,000. Gee, what's with Goku? Could he be a Super Saiyan? He reaches 180,000.

Episode 57. "Goku is Ginyu, and Ginyu is Goku!"

Frieza says to Guru, "You green blob!" Like I said before, I just have this thing about blobs.

Episode 61. "Password is Porunga" (Namek's Dragon).

A pink girl frog chases after Captain Ginyu in the frog's body.

> "Earth dragon balls are the size of fists.
> Namek dragon balls are the size of heads."
> —Sam of Washington D.C.

> "The Namek Dragon is huge and looks really evil and has four horns on his head."
> —Feefah of Brooklyn

Episode 62. "Piccolo's Return."

Do the veins actually pop on anyone's forehead? They're always bulging as if ready to pop through Piccolo's forehead.

Anyway, Piccolo returns to Namek for the first time. Under Vegeta's orders, Dendee requests immortal life for Vegeta. Porunga, the Namek Dragon, explodes and becomes dragon balls. Guru has died. So the dragon balls are now useless. Frieza's an ugly dude.

Episode 64. "Fighting Power: One Million?"

The transformed Frieza looks very cool, but he sure grunts a lot. Frieza has two black horns. Long ago, Vegeta's father gave Vegeta to Frieza.

Frieza killed King Vegeta and his army. Vegeta's father is now dead. Frieza destroyed the entire planet. Frieza is now transformed. He is so cool. His tail autowinds and goes out really far. His power is over 1 million. He creates tidal waves and floods.

Episode 65. "Gohan Attacks" (title of uncut version) or "Piccolo, the Super Namek" (title of censored version).

Dendee and Krillin emerge from the water. Krillin's okay after all, but so is Frieza. Two musical notes sound like the western cowboy music before a shootout.

Krillin throws Destructo Disks at Frieza. How can he be so strong after Frieza practically kills him?

A very funny part, according to Danny, is when Krillin sticks out his tongue and thrusts his rear end at Frieza.

Episode 66. "Déjà Vu."

Why are all the Namek trees so tall and thin with blue Afros on top like lollipops? Is there a tree on Earth that looks like a lollipop?

Piccolo is fighting Frieza. Nail shows up. Nail

happens to be inside Piccolo. Piccolo wants to fight Frieza alone. "Horn Boy" is what Piccolo calls Frieza. Lots of grunting by everyone.

Okay, now we come to a *Huge Turning Point Show*:

Episode 80. "Transformed at Last."

Goku turns into Super Saiyan Goku. Lots of water surrounds everybody because they're on a tiny island. A golden aura surrounds Goku. He has green eyes and blond hair. When the gold aura goes away, Goku's hair turns white.

Episode 81. "Explosion of Anger."

Matt explains, "There are five levels to Super Saiyan. When Goku gets to Level Five, his hair's *really* long."

This episode shows even more water explosions than in previous episodes. Frieza shoots tons of fire bombs. Goku survives all of the attacks, even ones that look like nuclear bombs.

Episodes 88 and 89. Danny likes these two episodes a great deal. Goku detransforms from Super Saiyan form. Frieza uses his little pink Destructo Disks, Goku dodges them, and they cut Frieza in thirds: an upper body, a lower body, and his left arm up to his shoulder. But Frieza comes back *again*. No matter. Goku finishes him off because he's weak. Because Goku is "the hope of the universe!"

Fast Fact Quiz!

Which Dragon Ball Z character never dies, not even once?

Answer 1: Goku
Answer 2: Mr. Satan
Answer 3: Piccolo
Answer 4: Buu

9

Dragon Ball Z Action Figures

"When you press Cell's shoe hard, he flies at you like a torpedo."
—Danny Gresh, coauthor of this book

"Why do their vests and arms fall off in one second? Is this some sicko plot to take over the world?"
—Important person who asked to remain anonymous

Let me start this chapter by telling you that I have many long years of experience playing with action figures. I am perhaps one of the world's greatest experts when it comes to action figures.

All of that, of course, is nonsense.

But I *do* like action figures, and we have plenty of them here. Danny and I often quibble over who gets to play with the toys. For example, one year, I got some *Mars Attacks* spaceships and alien guys. The spaceships came with torpedoes, and I was looking forward to a marvelous time, shooting those things all over the living room.

Danny got to my *Mars Attacks* toys before I could shoot my torpedoes even once! The cat was tormented for a while, but survived it all.

Dan and I have many Dragon Ball Z action figures. He's suffering right now because I have all of them here on my bed (where I'm writing this chapter), and so he can't play with them until

I finish this chapter. So I will now get on with it. After all, I hate to see my son suffer.

Basically, it seems that two companies offer these action figures. One is Irwin Toys, the other is Bandai from Japan. Most toy stores and media-type shops carry the action figures from Irwin. Some of the Bandai figures, however, are well worth seeking. For example, not much can beat my big, fat Majin Buu from Bandai. Sure, his purple cape falls off when you touch him (and I mean, when a piece of your hair floats near any part of his body, that's touching him). But he's just perfect. He looks very Buuish, and both his arms and legs are pliable—soft, not rigid and hard like the arms and legs on other action figures.

The smaller Dragon Ball Z figures are pliable, too, and they're pretty fun when you want to do some pretend-punching. They're also useful when you want to shoot Irwin's Blasting Energy Weapon Balls and knock them down.

These Blasting Energy Ball figures are some of the neatest action figures I've ever seen. Super Saiyan Goku comes with an energy ball that you stick into his hand. Then you press a button on his back, and bam, a row of small Dragon Ball Z guys fall down. You can pretend that the edge of your kitchen table is a cliff, and whack them all off so they fall into the whirling ocean below.

Vegeta comes with a Blasting Energy Ball, too. In his case, when you stick the ball into his hand, it looks as if both his hands are concentrating a huge power ball at an opponent. You slide a button on his back to the left, and off the ball goes.

If you set two of these guys up, facing each other, you can shoot the balls back and forth, and see which guy wins: Goku or Vegeta. Another neat thing you can do is have both Goku and Vegeta shoot their balls at the big green Cell action figure. When Cell is hit, his wings, tail, and arms fall off.

In fact, it seems as if all these guys lose body parts and clothing when they're hit hard enough. Here's what Danny has to say about all this:

"When hit with a ball, Super Saiyan Gohan's arms and shirt come off; same with Trunks. Super Saiyan Trunks' armor falls off, as well as his arms. When hit with a ball, Vegeta's hands, feet, and armor all come off. Thin Majin Buu's arms come off, but they're not as easy to stick back in as the arms of Super Saiyan Trunks. I think you'd have to run over Fat Majin Buu with a lawn mower to get his arms off. [*We don't recommend that you use the lawn mower approach.*—Lois] I just make all the little guys stand there when Cell is pounding on everybody else."

Captain Ginyu can hold his energy ball high, then twist his body while thrusting his arm and shooting his ball. Actually, you slide a button on his back to the left to shoot the ball, but overall, the spontaneous action of making this figure pose and move and then slam the ball at some other guys is really well done. The Ginyu energy ball figure is one of the best. Speaking of which, you can shift his legs around so he squats, kneels, turns in all sorts of bizarre positions, then slam the ball. When he's hit by another guy's ball, Ginyu immediately loses his armor and his eye visor.

Energy Ball Frieza is ridiculously cool. He has a long and very gross removable tail. But even better, you stick the energy ball in his mouth! His legs, feet, and tail (and of course, his arms and neck) move in all directions—this guy is really disgusting and funny! Good luck keeping his legs and feet on his body, though. As Jim, 10, likes to say:

"He looks like he's throwing up all the time, while he's wobbling around with no legs and only a chunk of tail sticking out of him."

Now I know that I'm focusing on the energy ball figures from Irwin, but they happen to be my favorites. I'll finish up by telling you about Piccolo, who as you might guess, is one of the best figures in the entire collection.

You stick the long pole energy thing into his hand (he's the only figure with a pole beam instead of an energy ball), then you twist his head or his right arm around until he fires the pole beam. You kind of have to see this one to believe it.

If you set Frieza against Piccolo, and maybe put Fat Majin Buu between them, good luck, you'll have quite a fierce battle going on your kitchen table or the floor of your bedroom. Or wherever your mother lets you play with these things. Personally, I like them battling on the furry rug in the living room. Or outside in the grass.

We could go on and on about the various Dragon Ball Z action figures. There are dozens of them. And I mean, dozens of tiny ones, dozens of medium-sized ones, and dozens of big ones. And even half a dozen giant ones. Right now, a huge (gawking, goofy-smiling) Goku is hovering over me from the bookshelf. Beside him, is a large and very cute Gohan. And next to Gohan is a miniature Oolong.

The miniatures are soft and come in tons of poses. You can take them with you anywhere you go simply because they're so tiny. And because they're so soft, you make believe that they're fighting by twisting their arms and legs all over.

The miniatures are excellent to use when you're participating in a role-playing game (see Chapter 10). For example, there are miniature Super Saiyan Gokus at different Super Saiyan power levels—one figure has thick, yellow hair, another has *really long* thick, yellow hair. When I was little, I would keep little figures like these in my desk at school, and in my backpack for screwing around on the bus. My friends and I once had a six-desk world set up with little figures—until our teacher caught us playing with them, so that was the end of that. I guess I'd recommend that you *not* stick them in your desks at school. But I never got in trouble for playing with my action figures on the school bus!

One thing you should know about these action figures is that there are some imitations floating around, and they're very weird looking. For example, instead of being pink, you might find a Majin Buu with a head that looks like the skin is made out of a grilled cheese sandwich. No kidding.

My final comment about all this is that I don't understand why Master Roshi has a giant turtle shell on his back. I know he lives in Kame House. I know he lives with a turtle. But still—! I know that Master Roshi's supposed to have a turtle shell on his back at all times, but come on, have you ever seen a guy with a gigantic shell glued to his entire back? Or even to part of his back? Or to his head as a hat? Master Roshi seems to spend a lot of time in the bathroom on the toilet. Goku calls to Master Roshi from the Other World (from death itself!), and of course, Master Roshi hears these calls from the dead while he's sitting on the toilet. Don't ask me, I don't know why Master Roshi is always on the toilet. Maybe it has something to do with that turtle shell on his back. Maybe there's a buffer device on the back of the toilet that oils and cleans his turtle shell, and maybe the shell requires 23 hours of oiling and cleaning every day.

Makes sense to me.

That's not much of a final comment, is it? Okay, I'll give you one more final comment. As you probably remember, I am Daniel's mother. Now, as a mother-woman type of person, as opposed to a guy, I do wonder why there's no ChiChi action figure. I do not miss having a Bulma figure, but the entire Bandai-Irwin series is really making me sad by not offering ChiChi.

I will say one more thing, then I promise we'll

move to the next chapter about the role-playing game. Okay, they did something silly with Master Roshi. Okay, they neglected to make a ChiChi for me. But what's this about no action figure of King Kai? And what about Bubbles the Monkey? For crying out loud, how can you expect to play Dragon Ball Z games with any flavor, any attitude, any fever—

If you don't have a Bubbles the Monkey?

Fast Fact Quiz!

Hey, what's the difference between an action character with yellow hair and one with gold hair?

Answer 1: The figures with yellow hair are wearing wigs.

Answer 2: The figures with gold hair are rich.

Answer 3: If you soak the yellow-haired action figures in water for ninety days straight, their hair will turn gold.

Answer 4: The first Dragon Ball Z Super Saiyan action figures were made with yellow hair. The first Dragon Ball GT Super Saiyan action figures were made with gold hair. When Bandai, the makers of the Dragon Ball Z action figures saw the gold hair of the GT figures, they got really jealous and switched the Dragon Ball Z hair to gold, too. Actually, Bandai made both the Z and GT figures, so they were jealous of themselves. Maybe Bandai had two guys making action figures, and they were big rivals. Maybe their names were Kami and Piccolo, or Thin Buu and Fat Buu. The other major action figure manufacturer, Irwin, makes Super Saiyans with yellow hair. Perhaps Irwin is just one guy named Irwin, so he never competes with himself by making gold hair or yellow hair. The simple answer: the Japanese figures have gold hair, the American ones have yellow hair.

10

Kamehameha! Choukamehameha! Martial Arts and Energy Blasts: The Role-Playing Game

"Isn't it kind of weird when Bulma returns young and sees Trunks, her own son? She actually asks her own kid if she looks beautiful being young. He says that she looks pretty much the same as when she's his much older mother. And that makes Bulma happy, because now she figures that she looks beautiful when she's old, too. She is *so* vain."
—Lois, coauthor of this book (I would *never* ask Danny such a stupid question!)

This chapter will present some simple examples of the Dragon Ball Z role-playing game. We'll talk a little more about ki, which we talked about in Chapter 2. As you might remember, ki is the internal energy used when a Dragon Ball Z character attacks something. We'll show you how to use it effectively during role-playing games.

You can also scream "Ki-ai" whenever you want, but probably not during a math test or during Thanksgiving meals at grandma's house. Ki-ai is the shriek made by Dragon Ball Z characters when they focus their ki.

These Dragon Ball Z guys are really weird.

> "If I went around shrieking Ki-ai constantly
> and staring into space, I'd get in a lot of
> trouble."
> —Eric the Invincible, age 10

True. Not to mention "Ha," the big grunt-shriek you hear from Dragon Ball Z guys while they're fighting each other.

> "If I went around shrieking Ki-ai constantly and staring into space, and then grunt-shrieking Ha at people, they'd throw me in jail."
> —the insane man by the bus stop

We made up that quote from the insane man by the bus stop. We just wanted to put him in the book. He was a guy who waved at us with three fingers while grunt-shrieking Ha from his position across the windshield of our car. No kidding. He scared us to death one dark night when we were trying to pry Danny's sister, Rena, from a flute session in a dilapidated building in the middle of nowhere. Rena tended to have flute sessions all over the planet; well, all over the city, but Danny and I had plenty of time to kill during these flute sessions, and stuff like buildings and insane men grew to immense proportions in our minds over the years. By the time Rena stopped hauling us around the city so she could play the flute everywhere, Dan and I had developed entire four-hour time-killing routines around our memory of the insane man. We still do it. We wave three fingers at each other and grunt-shriek Ha, and then laugh our heads off.

But I got off track again. I tend to do that.

I will now get very serious and adultlike again. That is an important thing to do. (I really don't know why, but I feel as if I'm supposed to say that every now and again, especially after telling you about the insane man and similar things. Though I really can't think of anything remotely similar to the insane man.)

In this chapter, we'll also tell you something about *ken*, and by that, we don't mean your sister's Barbie doll boyfriend. Rather, we're referring to the ken that means fist or technique, as described in the role-playing manual, *Dragon Ball Z The Anime Adventure: The Ultimate Martial Artists Battle for Control of the Cosmos!* This is the only book that we have about the role-playing game, and it serves as a reasonable starting point if you want to learn how to pretend as if you're in complex Dragon Ball Z adventures. You can find out more about it on the Internet at the official site of role-playing game book, *http://www.talsorian.com.*

Note that, in the role-playing book, the Raditz Saga means the same thing as the Saiyan Saga. Also, the role-playing book divides the series into slightly different sagas from the standard ones described in this book: Saiyan, Frieza, Androids from the Future, Cell Game, Majiin Buu. The main difference, of course, is that most fans we know don't think of the Cell Saga as being divided between Androids from the Future and Cell Game.

There's one more sound that characters make a lot. It's the sound of fear, something like "Err-err-ehh-ehh." We don't know the name of this sound, but Krillin says it constantly, and so does Gohan. They also use the "Err-err-ehh-ehh" sound when they're surprised.

Basically, when you do role playing, you pretend to be one or more characters, and so do your friends. Then you make up the game, speaking your lines as you make them up. In this particular role-playing game, you pretend to be Dragon Ball Z characters, you make up adventures, and you go on these adventures with your friends. You roll dice to figure out all your power levels, whether you win battles, and whether you gain strength.

When you create a character (or if the game-master lets you choose a character by rolling the dice), the first thing you do is determine the charactistics and skills.

Power Level—Roll two dice. The first represents the hundreds position, the second represents the tens position. So if you roll a four and a two, your Power Level is 420.

Characteristics

Physical, Mental, Combat, and Move—When you assign points to these categories, you have a maximum of 40 points. So you could put 10 points in Physical, 11 in Mental, 10 in Combat, and 13 in Move: you decide. Characters with a low Combat level are most likely to miss when they attack. For Power Up rate, you add Physical to Mental, then multiply the result by 10. For example, if Karunirin's Mental level is 11 and his Physical is 10, then his Power Up is 210. The character with the highest Mental number goes first in the game.

Skills

Fighting, Evasion, Weapon, Power, Body, Mind—When you assign points to these sections, you have 50 maximum points to place. After you do this, you add the Combat number to Fighting; this gives you the total value of the Fighting skill for your character. You then add the Combat number to the Evasion skill, which gives you the total value of Evasion. Then you repeat this process to get your totals for the Weapon and Power skills. Next, you add the Body number to the Physical number (see *Characteristics* above), and the result is the number you assign for the Body skill. Finally, you add the Mind number to the Mental number, and the result is the number you assign for the Mind skill.

Defense—Toughness of your character. Calculated by multiplying five by your Physical level. If another player hurts your guy, then you subtract Defense points from your player.

Hits—Typically thought of as Lives. In this case, it is calculated by multiplying 10 by your Physical level. Another way to calculate hits is to just double your Defense level. If another player hurts your guy, then damage is subtracted from your guy's hits until you have zero hits and lose the game.

When playing the game, you should consider the power levels of characters in the real show. This may help you develop adventures of your own. For example, when Raditz first arrives on Earth, his power level is 1,250, while Goku's is 332 before he removes his weights, Piccolo's is 321 before he removes his weights, and Gohan's fluctuates from one to 1,307 (when he gets really mad and bashes Raditz in the chest), depending on his emotional state.

A Few Role-Playing Game Facts and Tips

1. If you have ten sensu beans, you can restore all of your character's Hits (Lives).
2. Korin, the blue cat with the walking stick who doles out the sensu beans, would be a fun and challenging character to play, given that his only role is to give sensu beans to the other characters.
3. It's harder to play the role of Kami than Korin. This is very odd. However, according to the rules, Korin, a mere cat who does nothing but grow beans, has a Defense level of 80, whereas the all-mighty Kami, who trains Earth's greatest warriors, only has a Defense level of 50. Korin also has a higher fighting value (20) than Kami (15).
4. It might be fun to play a fighter such as Piccolo, but simultaneously, play the role of Korin and one or both of the Eternal Dragons. Shenlong has 300 Hits (Lives), far more than other characters. He also has a Defense level of 150, which is quite high. His Mental ability is 25, extremely high, even higher than Bulma's mental ability—and her Mental prowess exceeds

the Mental numbers of all the human and Saiyan-human characters. So a Dragon would be an interesting and powerful character to play.

5. Once again, I must come to the defense of Oolong the Pig. His Mental power is only three, and his Physical power is only four. It's a well-established fact that pigs are smarter than police dogs. So why is Oolong's brainpower so low? And given that he is a shapeshifting pig, shouldn't his Physical power be higher, as well? I suggest that you bend the rules and play Oolong the Pig with much higher powers in all categories.

6. Don't forget that, along with the fighters, you can play fun characters such as Oolong the Pig, mentioned above, or even Master Roshi's sister, Baba. She has a crystal ball, which you can use to predict the future (for example, who will win the next battle?) and to see what's going on in other places (for example, are your opponents en route to your hideout?). Be careful with Baba, though. She can easily be hit and destroyed. Her Mental level is only six, and her Physical ability is only two. Worse, her Combat level is set to one, as

low as you can go. She has only 20 Lives (Hits), so think twice before you toss her into battle!

7. Finally, I must mention Bubbles the Monkey. Somebody has to play Bubbles the Monkey. Sadly, he has no Power Up level; that's right, a big flat zero. His Mental skills are set at four, his Physical ability at 12. He has ample Lives (Hits) of 160. Personally, I'd give him a much higher Physical rating. After all, he gives guys like Goku a real workout—it's hard for the best warriors in the universe to catch Bubbles and beat him in the big chase games.

Frankly, there's no way to figure out how to play a good game without analyzing the official game book, and then practicing often by playing the game with your friends. We could easily devote three entire books to the rules. But we just want to give you a taste of the role-playing game here.

We start with a simple scenario that shows you the basics of creating a character. The second example shows how to play a very simple game, assuming that you've already set up the characters, and the third example is a slightly complex game.

First, we choose a gamemaster. He's the guy who will define the ground rules of our game and set the scene for the beginning of the game. He'll also record power levels and tell us if we're allowed to do what we want.

Naturally, in our case, Danny is the gamemaster. He immediately sets the scene:

"It's in the day around noon. It's humid and very hot."

I sigh at this point. I am thinking, oh dear, humid and very hot, that's the opening line of all bad fiction, including spoofs about bad fiction in the movies. However, Dan is ten and this is his story, he is the gamemaster, so I keep my mouth shut—after all, the weather is probably irrelevant to the game and we aren't writing the great American novel here, we're screwing around with action figures and doing the Dragon Ball Z role-playing game!—and Danny continues:

"It's in the mountains. At an abandoned ski resort. Abandoned because it's not winter. There's some guy burning chloroflourocarbons, one of our daily vocabulary words in school."

Ah, good, who cares about hot and humid? Danny's come up with chloroflourocarbons: the kid's going strong!

"Pay attention, Mom. The guy's burning the chloroflourocarbons inside an airtight dome. This way, he doesn't destroy the ozone layer."

I'm a real pain in the you-know-what, so I say:

"But Danny, *why* is the guy burning the chloroflourocarbons?"

He pauses. He thinks. Then he looks at me intently as if the answer is obvious. "Because," he says, "the guy has too many Styrofoam packing peanuts. He has to burn them. There's no other way to get rid of so many Styrofoam packing peanuts."

I nod. This makes perfect sense. "Continue," I say.

The room seems to get dark. His eyes almost glow. I am transfixed by the sound of his voice. Suddenly he grunt-shrieks, "Hu! Hu! Ha! Hu hu hu ha ha ai-ki hu!" and waves at me with three fingers.

No, I made that up. He doesn't do that.

Instead, he grunt-shrieks:

"There's a huge pit in the airtight dome, which is in the mountains where Dr. Wheelo's old fortress was. You can tell Goku was there because his shirt is on top of the mountain. You know how Goku always loses his shirts?"

"Yes, I sure do."

"Okay, so his shirt is hanging off the top of the mountain."

"Okay." Makes perfect sense.

"There's a heavily barricaded and locked door leading into the mountain.

"The bad guys want to destroy the world by getting through the barricaded door into the mountain, and from there, into the airtight dome. Then they plan to destroy the dome, releasing the burning chloroflourocarbons into the ozone layer. The Earth will be destroyed."

We decide that Dan is a character called HodgePodge. We decide further that I am also a new character called Oinky Chicken, who is Vegeta's cousin, an unknown Saiyan who has mysteriously arrived at the mountain.

We note that Yajirobe has a Mental power of seven, and that he's smarter than Goku at a Mental power of three. Weird. Yajirobe seems so lazy and dumb. Gohan's Mental power is also set to seven, which we also think is strange because he studies all the time and should be much smarter than Goku and Yajirobe. Bulma is the smartest, however, with a Mental power of 12, which makes sense since she's a super engineer.

And so, with all this in mind, we're ready to set the initial power levels of our characters. We decide that Oinky Chicken will have a Mental power of 12, equal to that of Bulma. We also decide to give Oinky Chicken a beginning Power Level of 420. Oinky Chicken's Combat level is five; this is because the Chicken part of the character has legs but no arms, and the Oinky part of the character doesn't fight. In terms of Physical strength, we give our character a setting of 10, because he can run fast due to his long Chicken legs, yet he has no other physical attributes that would make him fast or strong. For Movement, Oinky Chicken receives a setting of 40 minus 27, or 13.

Finally, we move on down the list and give Oinky Chicken his final settings:

Fighting = 10
Evasion = 11
Weapons = 5
Body = 10
Mind = 4
Power = 10

And now I insist upon giving my new character some special powers. Danny resists, but I think it's important for Oinky Chicken to have attacks suited to his characteristics, so here we go:

Special Powers	Extra Dice
Stink Bomb	10–12
Snort Peck Blast	5–7

Danny says that the dome itself will have a Defense setting of 120, with Hits, or Lives, set at 240.

And now we begin the first battle.

Oinky Chicken gathers Power, which means it's his turn. Because 12 plus 10 equals 22, we multiply 22 by 10 to yield 220 for Oinky Chicken's Power Up rate. He wants to blow up the dome with a Stink Bomb. HodgePodge fights Oinky Chicken. If HodgePodge wins, Earth is saved. If Oinky Chicken wins, Earth is going bye-bye because the chloroflourocarbons will be released from the dome.

Next, it's HodgePodge's turn, so he gathers Power, and then he walks toward Oinky Chicken.

Oinky Chicken throws a 220-point Stink Bomb attack at HodgePodge. His Combat number is five, his Power is 10, so we roll three dice. The characteristic is Combat, the skill is Power, and you have to add those two numbers to the rolls of three dice to beat the Difficulty value of the attack (which is determined by dividing the 220-point value of the Stink Bomb attack by 10), which is 22.

For this example, let's pretend that Oinky Chicken rolls three dice, and the rolls are one, six, and one. You add one plus six plus one to Combat (five) and Power (10), yielding a result of 23. This beats the Difficulty value of the attack. So in this particular case, Oinky Chicken's attack succeeds.

Oddly enough, Oinky Chicken rolls dice again. This time, he rolls 34 dice (22 due to the Difficulty value of his attack plus 12 extra because that's what the Stink Bomb Special Powers number dictates to us). He then adds all the numbers from all 34 dice. Let's pretend that adding all the dice numbers results in a total of 147.

If HodgePodge has a Defense of 75, then 75 of the 147 points bounce off his Defense. Because he has a Defense of 75, he automatically has Hits of 150 (because as mentioned earlier, Hits are double the Defense). So the other 72 points are subtracted from his Hits of 150, giving him 78 Hits (Lives) left.

One more thing, as if all of the above wasn't enough to confuse you into wanting to leap to the bottom of a quicksand pit. When trying to beat the Difficulty value, if you happen to roll all ones, your attack automatically fails.

You can already see that as you begin to play a game, it quickly becomes extremely complicated. For example, we just tossed in the definition of the Difficulty value to show you how to figure out whether a character's attack succeeds.

For one of the ways to get around rolling the dice, it says in the role-playing guide that we can multiply the final number by three. Goku's Spirit Bomb supposedly receives an infinite number of dice rolls, so you could perhaps roll the dice 10 times and multiply the final number of any gigantic number, and then it's goners to the bad guys without thinking much about it.

In short, some of the role-playing game rules seem a bit odd to us.

We now present a second simple role-playing game, this one created totally by Danny one night after school. He rolled all the dice, he added and subtracted and multiplied, etc., all the resulting numbers. Then he summarized the game for you without including all the dice rolls (because that would make this chapter 350 pages long and incomprehensible unless you happen to be Albert Einstein or some other mathematical wizard).

Karunirin the Saiyan is facing Ladon from Earth. Since Ladon's Mental power is 12 to Karunirin's 11, he goes first.

Gamemaster: Phase 1. Ladon, you start.

Ladon [to the Gamemaster]: Hold my power down to 150. (When Karunirin uses his scouter on Ladon, Karunirin won't be able to read Ladon's true power level, which is much higher at 510.) Now I use a scouter to get a reading on Karunirin.

Gamemaster: You get a reading of 510. (Both characters apparently have the same power levels.)

Karunirin: I look around. Is there unusual terrain, or is this area flat?

Gamemaster: It's just a flat area. Ready? Phase 2.

Ladon: I raise some power.

Karunirin: Me, too.

Gamemaster: Phase 3, coming up.

Ladon: I rush at Karunirin and hit him with a Flame Slash.

Karunirin: I evade . . .

Gamemaster: Okay, roll the dice.

Ladon: No!

Gamemaster: Okay, Ladon misses on his attack. Karunirin?

Karunirin: Since he's close to me, I'll throw a flurry of punches.

Gamemaster: Roll. You hit. The number's 77. All but 75 punches just bounce off his

Defense. You cause no knockback at all. Okay. Phase 4.

Ladon: I raise Power. I'm at 570.

Karunirin: I raise Power, too. This takes me to 420. I boost my actions. I now show the gamemaster that I want three extra actions for a cost of 45. I'm at 375 now.

Gamemaster: Okay. Round 2, phase 1.

Ladon: I get back all of my Hits, tough luck, Karunirin. Now I'll keep on raising energy . . .

Karunirin: Okay, three extra actions. Action 1, I punch you. Actions 2, 3, and 4, I hit you with Flaming Kicks. Hiiiiiiiiiiaaaaaaaaaah!

Gamemaster: Okay. Roll to see if you hit. Your punches do 82 hits, and your Flaming Kicks do 59, 56, and 55. So, in all, that is 252. Your Defense shaves 90 from that, but you still take 162 points. Okay, round 2, phase 2.

Ladon: Aaaah! I have one point left! I'll raise a deflection—I am raising a 500-point deflection, and I'll rest.

Karunirin: That deflection isn't going to do much good, buster. I punch you!

Gamemaster: You deliver 90 points. Since Ladon has one left, he is knocked out good.

Karunirin: All right, Mr. Gamemaster, now it's your turn. Hahahahahahahaha!

And now we present our final sample game. While this one pushes us a bit further into the world of a role-playing game, like the previous two examples, it's still pretty simple. You have to play the Dragon Ball Z game a lot to get really good at it. Practice!

Announcer: Welcome all, who will challenge each other in this battle. First, we have the Saiyan, Karunirin, from the outer reaches of space, to show us his power. He likes to wipe people out and give the remains to the cockroaches. He has died before and learned up to the Kaio Ken times four from King Kai. Next we have Ladon, a human. Strong and determined to win, he will be with us today. Now we have John. He may not look like much, but he can pack a punch. Lastly, Bordome is here. He's a Saiyan who values everything . . . about himself. LET THE BATTLE BEGIN!

Gamemaster: Phase 1. Ready, Bordome is first.

Bordome: I use my scouter on John to see if I can get a reading.

Gamemaster: You get a reading of 640.

Bordome: (whistles)

Ladon: I look around. Are there distinct features or is this place flat?

Gamemaster: You see mountains all around. There's a dome on top of one mountain. A man's burning chloroflourocarbons in the dome. You see dark clouds gathering. A boulder's perched precariously on a ledge above Bordome. The boulder weighs, oh, let's say two tons, so if it fell, Bordome would have to roll 100 dice to determine his damage.

Karunirin: How far apart are we?

Gamemaster: Everyone is about 2,000 yards away from one another.

John: Can I get a reading on Bordome using my scouter?

Gamemaster: You get a reading of 110.

John: Whoa, no sweat there!

Gamemaster: Okay. Phase 2!

Bordome: Let's see about that, puny boy. I think I'll raise some Power this phase.

Gamemaster: You can hear the wind begin to howl and the ground shakes slightly as Bordome gathers energy.

Ladon: I will raise Power, also.

Karunirin: I will raise Power.

John: Raising Power here.

Gamemaster: Phase 3.

Bordome: I'll fly mach 1 for 10 minutes, getting closer to Ladon.

Ladon: I'll fly mach 4 for 10 minutes, too, moving away.

Karunirin: I'll use a Kaio Ken times four to increase my Power. I'm at 1,050.

John: I'll fly mach 4 for 20 minutes, coming up on Bordome.

Gamemaster: Phase 4.

Bordome: I whirl around and hit John with a 250-point blast. Yaaah!

Gamemaster: It does 82 points of damage. You fall out of the sky and crash onto the ground. Take another 10 dice.

John [rolls 10 dice to determine his damage]: Only does 36 damage and bounces off my defense.

Ladon: I land and sprint away.

Karunirin: I'll hit with a 300-point energy attack on Bordome and I'll aim it directly at him! Garrick Gun! Yaaah, 386 points!

Gamemaster: Since it's 386, Bordome, your defense brings it down to 311, but your Hits are only 150. So, you are dead.

John: I will boost my Actions to five and
Power Up. (This means that John will do
five things during his next turn.)

Gamemaster: Round 2, phase 2.

Ladon: I'll Power Up.

Karunirin: I'll raise a 600 deflection, so I'm
down to 250 in Power.

John: Okay. Action 1, I get up. Action 2, I zip
up to Karunirin. Actions 3, 4, 5, I punch
him.

Gamemaster: Only one of your flurries of
punches hit him, delivering 48 points of
damage, not enough to injure. Round 2,
phase 2.

Ladon: I'll sprint again.

Karunirin: I see Ladon sprinting. I blast him
with a 250-point Garrick Gun.

Gamemaster: You do 166 damage. He takes 91
points of damage.

John: I think I'll hit him with a 180-point
Thunder Blast.

Gamemaster: It does 50 because of Ladon's defense. He is down to nine. Round 2, phase
3.

Ladon: I raise a 700-point deflection.

Karunirin: I'll gather Power.

John: Me, too.

Gamemaster: Round 2, phase 4.

Ladon: I sprint.

Karunirin: I use Kaio Ken times 10.

Gamemaster: It nearly blows apart your body, but you hang on.

John: I raise Power.

Gamemaster: Round 3, phase 1.

Ladon: I rest.

Karunirin: I open up with a 1,100-point Garrick Gun on Ladon.

Gamemaster: You hit and deliver 623 points, which splash on his deflection, lowering it. His shield reflects into a mountain and blows the mountain to pieces. You can see people scurrying around where the mountain used to be.

John: I'll raise Power.

Gamemaster: Round 3, phase 2.

Ladon: I blast another mountain into bits.

Karunirin: I still have a lot left, so I'll hit you with a 650-point Flaming Kick.

Gamemaster: You deliver 287 points. He takes 212. He is knocked out cold.

John: I use a Thunder Blast on Karunirin that is 700 points.

Gamemaster: You deliver 269, but it reflects off his deflection and slams you. John, you are dead.

Post-Game Analysis: Judging by the numbers,

Bordome should have won this game. He had a tremendous edge in Power, physically and mentally. Not to mention his Power Up level. But instead, he got overconfident and wasn't aware of his surroundings. He could have stopped Karunirin after he used the Kaio Ken. But he used his Power on Ladon, who neither had a good Evasion nor decent Power skill. Karunirin won the game.

Fast Fact Quiz!

Can you cheat in the role-playing game by having lots of capsules that give you unlimited weapons and lives?

Answer 1: yes
Answer 2: no
Answer 3: probably
Answer 4: possibly

11

Dragon Ball Z Trading Cards

"There are three ways to lose the Cell Game: fall out of the ring, give up, or die. Guess that last one is pretty obvious, huh?"

—Joe Shmoe, randomly selected man on the streets of New York City, chosen for a Dragon Ball Z interview because he was karate-chopping blocks of wood while heel-kicking the windows of the World Trade Center Building.

Dragon Ball Z cards are sold in many countries: Japan (of course), the United States, Spain, and France, to name a few. There are literally thousands of Dragon Ball Z and GT cards.

We have Series 1, 2, and 3, in the English language. And also some from Japan, which seem to have different pictures and phrases from the ones printed in the United States.

The Japanese trading cards seem to come in three flavors: Dragon History, Versus Fight, and Gekisen Saikyo Quiz. We were lucky to have Yutaka Morita help us translate a few of these cards. We wanted you to see the kinds of things Japanese kids see when they play with their trading cards. Mr. Morita points out that the Japanese is probably particular to an area of Japan or to the way children talk. So his translations may be a little different from the original meanings.

But it's great fun to take a look at these cards.

For example, three of our Japanese trading cards include these lines:

DRAGON HISTORY
(Will Buu be finished at last?) Lock up Buu with with Successive Super Doughnuts and blast away with Crashing Ultra Buu Volleyball!

VERSUS FIGHT
(Bejit beats Buu) Earth-shaking ultimate battle with devilish Buu, whose power has been strengthened by absorbing Gohan.

GEKISEN SAIKYO QUIZ
Gekisen! Saikyo Quiz (Fierce battle! Most powerful quiz) Q: What is the instrument Daikaiohjin has given to Goku in order to join Goku and Vegeta together? Answers: Borata, Botari, or Botara?

There are probably other types of Japanese trading cards, as well as categories other than Dragon History, Versus Fight, and Gekisen Saikyo Quiz. These are the only types we've seen. If you know anything else about the Japanese cards, visit us on the Internet at *http://www.sff.net/ people/lgresh/DragonballZ.html*, and tell us what you know.

Of the English trading cards, as mentioned

earlier, we have Series 1, Series 2, and Series 3. All come from FUNimation, which also makes the English-language videos.

Series 1 cards come with a hologram card in each pack of 10 cards. They were released in 1996 from Bird Studio/Shueisha, Toei Animation.

Each Series 1 card includes the line, *Is it Defeat or Victory that Waits in the Dark*? The first card, Number 1, reads, "Dragon Ball Z. The Z team soldiers, along with Goku, try to save the Earth."

Aren't they always trying to do that? In every saga, every episode, every movie, every comic?

Series 1 seems to take us through the Raditz Saga. As numbered sequentially (that means, in order) from one up, the cards don't follow the exact storyline of the episodes and comics. They come pretty close, but shuffle the order here and there.

For example, Card 6 is: "Responding to Raditz' attack, Goku counterattacks using the Kamehameha Wave, but even that didn't work." Then Card 7 is: "The mighty Saiyan warrior Raditz arrives on Earth searching for his brother who had been sent to Earth as a baby." Clearly, 7 happened before the events of Card 6.

By the way, do you see something wrong with

Card 6? It should read: "Responding to Raditz' attack, Goku counterattacks using the Kamehameha Wave, but even that *doesn't* work."

The tenth card is very strange. "In place of my father I will keep the peace on Earth." "Hello, everybody!" That's exactly what's on the card. Who says which line?

According to Dan, our expert (at least in this house), Goku says both lines. Only Goku appears on the tenth card, unless you count the Dragon that he's standing on.

Card 59 indicates that "Gohan, enduring solitaire training for half a year, has increased in strength both mentally and physically." This is funny because it implies that Piccolo was training Gohan to play excellent solitaire games.

Series 2 cards also come in packs of 10. Instead of hologram cards, each pack contains one gold-foil card. In every 12 packs, you'll find one clear card, as well. Series 2 starts with the number one. The gold-foil cards are also numbered, starting with one, except their numbers have the letter G next to them. Oddly enough, every gold-foil card says exactly the same thing: "The battle for the soldiers continue to carry out with the power of love, hatred, pity and anger." This series seems to trace the Vegeta saga.

Series 3 packs come with a gold metallic card,

which is different from a gold-foil card. As with Series 2, the gold cards in Series 3 are numbered starting with one, and each has a G next to it. All the regular cards are numbered starting with one, as well. In every 12 packs of Series 3 cards, you'll also find a clear card.

Series 3 focuses on the Frieza Saga. Because Frieza is my favorite evil character, I like this series of cards best. Besides, the art is beautiful on each card—way beyond cartoonlike drawings with simple color, these cards have lush artwork and very rich colors.

Every card in the series contains the line, "Love, hatred, pity and anger burst forth as the warriors continue to battle right versus wrong."

Unlike gold cards in Series 2, the Series 3 gold cards each have an additional line. For example, G-7 says, "A confident Piccolo, having removed his weighted clothing, challenges Frieza to battle."

If you're having trouble finding Dragon Ball Z trading cards, go to the FUNimation (*http://www.dragonballz.com*) or Japanimation Websites (*http://www.japanimation.com*), where they carry extensive amounts of Dragon Ball Z stuff.

Fast Fact Quiz!

Baba is:

Answer 1: an infant in a baby buggy
Answer 2: a lamb
Answer 3: a duck
Answer 4: none of the above

12

Video Games, Music, and More!

"I wonder if they have a clock from which
Gohan comes out and says, 'Cuckoo'."
—Tony, age 18

"I wonder if they have underpants for Monday
through Friday with Yamcha on them."
—anonymous girl (maybe Bulma)

"I wonder if they have any books called
Dragon Ball Z?"
—Marc Resnick, editor of this book called
Dragon Ball Z

I started an earlier chapter by telling you that I was going to write about episodes, movies, and then cut versus uncut material. Then I wrote about those topics in reverse order. Remember?

I'm going to do it again.

This time, I want to write about *AND MORE!* first, just because it seems like a funny thing to do.

More than what? We don't know yet! That's what makes it funny. Well, it's funny to me, but then, I'm just a goofy writer of cartoon books who watches *Beverly Hillbillies* reruns.

So we're doing it backward. *AND MORE!* This refers to all the stuff you see in stores and everywhere on the Internet.

Danny and I, for example, have some Dragon Ball Z T-shirts, which is no big deal. But man, we've seen all kinds of stuff around town, and I mean *everywhere around town*. Wall clocks and wristwatches. Posters and playing cards. Backpacks, stickers, keychains—say, what kid uses keychains anyway? Especially keychains with huge Goku glow-in-the-dark heads on them? I think these giant Goku keychains are really night-lights in disguise.

What else? Name it. Hats, boxer shorts (that's underwear that looks like shorts), piggy banks. Maybe the weirdest things we found were the Dragon Ball Z whiskey shot glasses. These must be for Master Roshi and nobody else. I notice that FUNimation, Japanimation, and other sites that specialize in anime like Dragon Ball Z don't sell whiskey shot cartoon glasses. Okay, what kid uses gigantic keychain-head-things? That's weird enough, but . . . absolutely no kid uses whiskey shot glasses, that I know for a fact!

One neat thing we found at a toy store was a series of Dragon Ball Z walkie talkies. The walkie talkie units look like Goku, Piccolo, Vegeta, and Frieza.

We've now officially ended the *AND MORE!* part of this chapter.

While writing *AND MORE!*, I've been listening to the Dragon Ball Z soundtrack. The music, according to the CD case, is by Shuki Levy and Kussa Mahehi.

The first track on the CD is the title music heard as the cartoon episodes begin. I really enjoy this song, which is actually called, "Main Title." You can hear guys grunting and making all sorts of fighting noises. I never notice all these noises while watching the cartoon.

I almost hate to admit it, but I also listen to "Main Title" at work in my half-cube. Nobody knows this little fact except you.

Then I listen to the rest of the CD (but "Main Title" is my favorite song).

The second track of the CD, "The Arrival of Raditz," begins with some sweet flute music. Danny's sister, Rena, plays the flute really well, so I always enjoy the flute opening of "The Arrival of Raditz." Then, quickly, the second song gets really dark and reminds me of *The Phantom of the Opera* music. If you've never seen *The Phantom of the Opera*, it's a play about this sad and kind of crazy guy (The Phantom) who scares people all the time, though all he really wants is to love some woman who's in plays and sings beautifully in the theater where he lives. Yes, he lives in the theater, beneath it to be exact, and "The Arrival of Raditz" music is much like the eerie organ music The Phantom plays to "haunt" his theater. Finally, "The Arrival of Raditz" starts sounding like PlayStation music, and I'm no longer scared thinking about *The Phantom of the Opera*.

The third song, "The World's Strongest Team," reminds me of a barbarian movie. My father used to watch original Hercules movies, and I had a fondness for Conan comics when I was in high school. Comics don't come with soundtracks, I know, I know, but I have a pretty crazy imagination, and I could almost hear the pounding music as I read those comics. Same stuff as the Hercules soundtracks. Scary, ominous, giving you the feeling that something creepy is about to happen.

The fifth and sixth songs (I'm skipping number four, as well as some others because you probably don't want to read about every single song on the CD!) are pretty good. They're scary and exciting, and you can almost see Gohan and Krillin flying around, clenching their fists, gasping in horror, and then facing a battle with Vegeta. Although I don't think these songs play during battles with Vegeta! Rather, these songs play while Gohan is learning how to survive on his own and while Goku's traveling down Snake Way to King Kai's house.

The seventh song reminds me of going to a professional hockey or baseball game. You know the music they play on the organ there to get you all excited about your team? The seventh song sounds like that, and also has more video game type music in it.

One more song is worth mentioning. In the background of this song, I hear some trumpet music that sounds oddly enough just like Danny's trumpet lesson this week. Wait! That is Danny. He's practicing his trumpet while I write this chapter.

Okay, so the ninth song, the one I wanted to tell you about, doesn't have elementary school trumpet music in it. But it does have a fragment that sounds very similar to: *This old man, he plays one, he plays knick-knack on my thumb.*

There are other Dragon Ball CDs available, though we only have one, the soundtrack we just discussed. There may be a Best of Dragon Ball CD; I've read about it on the Internet, though I've never seen it. I also don't know what it contains—Dragon Ball Z's musical greatest hits? If you happen to have this CD, please write to me and tell me about it.

We have a final topic in this chapter: video games. There are numerous Dragon Ball Z video games for the PlayStation. However, none are available in English versions.

You can hack up your PlayStation and install special Japanese translation chips, all required just to run the PlayStations CDs in your English machines, but frankly, I don't think it's worth doing. I'm going to wait for a Dragon Ball Z video game that doesn't require that I hack up my PlayStation. Most likely, nobody will release such a game, but oh well.

From what I know, the Dragon Ball Z video games are fighting games. In some games, you use power meters and special attacks.

At the Internet Website *http://vidsource. clever. net/psx/dbzl.htm*, you can view screenshots from a video game called *Dragon Ball Z Legends*, made in Japan by Bandai. Apparently, the game is a classic punch-kick-knock 'em out kind of match between opponents. From the screenshots, it looks like loads of fun, and you can set up the games so two guys fight one guy, three guys fight three guys, and so forth.

To learn more about Dragon Ball Z stuff, you might take a look at these (and other) places on the Internet:

Http://www.dragonballz.com The official Dragon Ball Z Website. Here, you can quickly find out about new Dragon Ball Z videos. For example, I learned from the official site that two videos are being released very soon: *TRUNKS: Mysterious, and Youth* and *TRUNKS: Prelude to Terror*. You can also read detailed descriptions about all the characters and episodes here, and view lots of Dragon Ball Z pictures.

Http://www.viz.com The place that makes the comic books. It includes episode and character information, late-breaking news about the comics, and lots of Dragon Ball Z pictures. In fact, there are Dragon Ball Z pictures all over the Internet. Danny and I have seen many hundreds of pictures, and we're not even trying to find them.

Http://www.anotheruniverse.com A great place online that will send you Dragon Ball Z action figures and videos. Of course, you have to pay for the stuff first. It goes without saying that you have to ask your parents for permission.

Http://www.dragonball.net One of many Websites that displays links to other Dragon Ball Z fan sites. This site happens to be one of the very best. You get the usual stuff here: information about episodes and characters, plenty of pictures. You can also vote for your favorite characters and shows, and send Dragon Ball Z email cards to your friends.

Http://www.talsorian.com The official Website of the company that published the role-playing guide. They don't tell you how to play the game here, but you can order the book from this site and read a summary of the game. Also included are online Websites devoted to the role-playing game, all of which are far more sophisticated than the examples we gave you in this book.

Http://www.irwin-toy.com The official Website of the company that makes the American versions of the action figures—you can't buy the toys at the online site, but it's interesting just to go there and sort of "touch" the place that makes Dragon Ball Z action figures.

** In case your parents are worried about you cruising around the Internet, looking for Dragon Ball Z Websites, tell them to read the following part of the book. You should read it, too! **

Danny and I have never really discussed Internet rules. He often goes online using my Internet account, and he searches for material to use in his homework and other school projects. He once found a huge Website devoted to all the known types of sheep in the world. He wrote an amazing report that month about sheep, and he included sheep photos that he downloaded from the huge Website. What you have to keep in mind when you quote material from the Internet is that you must give credit to the Website source of your material. With the photos, Danny supplied the Web address for the sheep site in his report.

Use the Internet only if your parents are supervising you or give you free access to it. Often, parents set limitations to their children's Internet use. This means the kids can only see stuff that kids *should* see. If you're a parent reading this section of the book, realize that you can set filters that limit your child's access to Internet material. If you're a kid reading this section of the book, ask your parents for permission and help with the Internet.

Fast Fact Quiz!
The Lower World is called:

Answer 1: Home for Idiotic Losers
Answer 2: House for Insane Lunatics
Answer 3: House for Intricate Losers
Answer 4: Home for Infinite Losers

APPENDIX A

Glossary

"I hope they never give us the names of energy attacks on spelling tests."
—Vera, age 10

This is a short glossary of terms that we thought you might be interested in reading. Some are Japanese words that correspond to English words for standard Dragon Ball Z terms; examples are the words meaning catch on fire, set on fire, and healing.

Anime. Cartoons.

Bugei. Japanese word for martial arts.

Chikara. Japanese word for strength, force, power.

Dragon ball. One of seven magical balls that summons the Eternal Dragon, who grants one wish to the person who collected the balls and uttered the special Dragon-summoning chant.

Furyoku. Japanese word for the force of the wind.

Ha. What a Dragon Ball Z character screams when releasing an energy blast.

Hi. Japanese word for a fire.

Hi ga tsuku. Japanese word for catch on fire.

Hi o tsukeru. Japanese phrase for set on fire.

Hiro. Japanese word for hero.

Kaio Ken. The technique that King Kai teaches to Goku, and which Goku uses to defeat many opponents. One of Goku's most famous power bombs.

Kame. Japanese word for turtle.

Kamehameha. Goku's trademark power bomb.

Ki. A character's internal energy.

Kintoun. Goku's nimbus cloud.

Manga. Comic books.

Nyoibo. Goku's Power Pole, the kung fu rod.

Saibamen. Grotesque robotic vegetablelike fighting creatures.

Saiyan. Strong race of people from the planet Vegeta.

Scouter. Eye gear that enables Saiyans to determine everyone else's power levels.

Senshi. Japanese word for warrior.

Sensu beans. Each bean has the power to heal a person who's been hurt in any way, including near-fatal injuries.

Snake Way. Long path that starts at the gate from our world and stretches to The Other Dimension. It ends beneath King Kai's planet.

Tairyoku. Japanese word for physical strength.

Tatakai. Japanese word for battle.

Tatakau. Japanese word for battling.

Uchu. Japanese word for the universe or entire cosmos.

Zensekai. Japanese word for the entire world.

Zenryoku. Japanese word for all of someone's power, their best effort.

APPENDIX B

Cheat Sheet

ANSWERS TO FAST FACT QUIZZES

Chapter 1.

A yoikominiminkminiminken is a:

Answer 1: ridiculous make-believe name of an attack

Chapter 2.

The Nameks are based on what animals?

Answer 3: Snails and slugs.

Chapter 3.

Nappa had hair once in:

Answer 4: The Bardock TV special.

Chapter 4.

What King Kai joke was cut from the censored version of Episode 55?

Answer 1: What vegetable gives you gas when you eat it in the morning? Asparagas!

Chapter 5.

Trunks is:

Answer 4: none of the above

Chapter 6.

If only King Kai could survive the 10,000 miles of Snake Way centuries ago, how do all of Goku's friends make the trip so easily?

Answer 4: I don't know!

Chapter 7.

What is the name of Piccolo's father?

Answer 3: Piccolo-Daimaou.

Chapter 8.

Which Dragon Ball Z character never dies, not even once?

Answer 2: Mr. Satan.

Chapter 9.

Hey, what's the difference between an action character with yellow hair and one with gold hair?

Answer 4: The first Dragon Ball Z Super Saiyan action figures were made with yellow hair. The first Dragon Ball GT Super Saiyan action figures were made with gold hair. When Bandai, the makers of the Dragon Ball Z action figures saw the gold hair of the GT figures, they got really jealous and switched the Dragon Ball Z hair to gold, too. Actually, Bandai made both the Z and GT figures, so they were jealous of themselves. Maybe Bandai had two guys making action figures, and they were big rivals. Maybe their names were Kami and Piccolo, or Thin Buu and Fat Buu. The other major action figure manufacturer, Irwin, makes Super Saiyans with yellow hair. Perhaps Irwin is just one guy named Irwin, so he never competes with himself by making gold hair or yellow hair.

Chapter 10.

Can you cheat in the role-playing game by having lots of capsules that give you unlimited weapons and lives?

Answer 1: Yes

Chapter 11.

Baba is:

Answer 4: none of the above

Chapter 12.

The Lower World is called:

Answer 4: Home for Infinite Losers.

Tell us what you like about this book! Tell us what you like about Dragon Ball Z, something about your favorite characters and episodes. Want to talk about the comic books or the action figures? We're available! And we love Dragon Ball Z as much as you do. So get in touch with us! Find us on the Internet at *http://www.sff.net/people/lgresh/DragonballZ.html*.

For general material about the Dragon Ball Z role-playing game, we used the following reference:

Dragon Ball Z The Anime Adventure—The Ultimate Martial Artists Battle for Control of the Cosmos!, by Mike Pondsmith with material adapted from Cindy Fukunaga of FUNimation Productions.

FIND OUT EVERYTHING YOU NEED
TO KNOW TO MASTER
THE WORLD'S FAVORITE
HAND-HELD GAME

HOW TO BECOME A POKÉMON MASTER

By Hank Schlesinger

It's all here. Amaze your friends, astound your parents, and impress your classmates with the valuable expert tips that can turn you into a champion Pokémon player. And you'll get them straight from the source: kids just like you who have played for hours on end and discovered the amazing secrets of this awesome game! Author Hank Schlesinger—an avid video game junkie himself—has interviewed kids who love Pokémon, and thrown in his own insights and tips, to create the ultimate Pokémon guide.

WITH SPECIAL BONUS TIPS FOR
OTHER GAME BOY GAMES

**An Unauthorized Guide—
Not Endorsed by Nintendo**

AVAILABLE WHEREVER BOOKS ARE SOLD
FROM ST. MARTIN'S PRESS

GET THE HOTTEST TIPS ON WINNING TODAY'S COOLEST VIDEO GAMES

HOW TO WIN AT NINTENDO 64 GAMES
Hank Schlesinger

Discover essential expert tips to help you win
at Nintendo 64.

HOW TO WIN AT SONY PLAYSTATION GAMES
Hank Schlesinger

Learn awesome expert tips to help you
ace Sony Playstation.

HOW TO BECOME A POKÉMON MASTER
Hank Schlesinger

Master the mega-popular game of monster collecting that
has spawned a cartoon series, comic books, and hundreds
of other toys.

schles6/99